THE STEP BY STEP ART OF
Ribbon Crafts

THE STEP BY STEP ART OF
Ribbon Crafts

Text and Ribbon Craft Designs by
ANITA HARRISON

CHARTWELL
BOOKS, INC.

Published by

CHARTWELL BOOKS, INC.
A Division of
BOOK SALES, INC.
110 Enterprise Avenue
Secaucus, New Jersey 07094

CLB 3309
© 1994 CLB Publishing, Godalming, Surrey, England
Printed and Bound in Singapore by Tien Wah Press
ISBN 0-7858-0068-9

AUTHOR'S ACKNOWLEDGEMENTS
Many thanks to Doug, my mother and father, Janet,
Caroline and my aunt for their patience and support,
and to my grandmother, who would have been so proud
to have seen this book.

PUBLISHER'S ACKNOWLEDGEMENTS
The publishers would like to thank the following
companies for supplying properties for photography:
pp. 21-22 Indian Ocean Trading Company,
28 Ravenswood Road, London SW12 9PJ;
pp. 30-31, 34-35, 52 All Good Gifts, 65 Northcote
Road, Battersea, London SW11 1NP; pp. 34-35, 53
Nice Irma's Ltd, 46 Goodge Street, London W1;
pp.64-65 Carvela Shoes Ltd, 67 New Bond Street,
London W1Y 9DF; pp. 44-45, 58-59, 80-81, 64-65,
Staks Trading Ltd, 31 Thames Street, KT1 1PH.

The author and the publishers are grateful to the
following companies for their generous help in
supplying ribbon for the projects in this book:
C.M. Offray & Son Ltd, Fir Tree Place, Church
Road, Ashford, Middlesex TW15 2PH; Panda
Ribbons (Selectus Ltd), The Uplands,
Biddulp, Stoke-On-Trent FT8 7RH.

Managing Editor: Jo Finnis
Editor: Adèle Hayward
Design: Claire Leighton; Nigel Duffield
Photography: Steve Tanner
Illustrations: Geoff Denney Associates
Typesetting: Andrew Tidy
Production: Ruth Arthur; Sally Connolly;
Neil Randles; Karen Staff; Jonathan Tickner
Director of Production: Gerald Hughes

Contents

Materials

Before starting any project you will need to read through the steps carefully in order to make a note of the materials needed. Total ribbon and fabric requirements are given either at their first mention in each project or at the back of the book.

Ribbons and Fabric

There is an enormous variety of **ribbon** available from department stores, haberdasheries and craft stores. They range from paper to moiré taffeta and sheer ribbon, and from plain colours to tartans, patterned gold braid and beaded ribbon. **Wire-edged ribbon** is particularly useful as it will hold its shape.

If you want to be more adventurous and choose a different pattern or colour of ribbon, make sure you use ribbon of the same fabric and width as specified. Ignoring this important point will lead to disappointment with the finished product. Choose **sewing thread** to match the ribbon as closely as possible for a professional finish.

The embroideries and tapestries are worked on a variety of **fabrics** and **canvases,** available from haberdashery and craft stores. Take care to follow thread ratios given for these.

Interfacing is required for several of the projects and it is important to adhere to the weights recommended. For weaving projects, always use **iron-on interfacing** in order to hold the ribbons in place at the back of the work.

Craft and Floral Accessories

Cards with pre-cut apertures, crêpe paper and **cotton moulds,** used to make the gift cards, sunflowers and the berries in the fruit and the garland, are available from craft stores.

Pearl-headed stamens are used for the flower centres and are available from craft and haberdashery stores (if you can only find stamens with a pearl each end, cut off one of the pearls).

Stub wire, fine floral wire, green wire and **paper florist's tape,** used in the making of the flowers, are all available from florists and garden suppliers as are **globe oases** and **block dry foam oases.**

Equipment

For Cutting

Sharp scissors are the most important piece of equipment for ribbon crafts and it is preferable to have a range of them at your disposal.

You will need a sharp pair of long-bladed **fabric scissors** for fabric or ribbons, and a pair of long-bladed **paper scissors** for paper and for ribbon treated in PVA medium. Use each pair for its respective purpose as using fabric scissors for cutting paper will blunt the blades. It is also handy to have a pair of small, sharp **embroidery scissors** for snipping threads and embroidery ribbons, and for other fine cutting work. **Pinking shears** are useful for cutting fabric and ribbon edges to prevent them from fraying.

While you can cut card with paper scissors, you will achieve a smoother edge using a **craft knife.**

For Sewing

For a large proportion of the projects you will require a sewing needle of some sort.

Fine **sewing needles** with eyes large enough to take a double strand of sewing thread are very handy, but if you are embroidering with narrow ribbons you will need a blunt-pointed **tapestry needle** with an eye large enough to thread the ribbon through. For the wall hanging only you will need a large **blunt needle** with the biggest eye available.

A sharp-pointed instrument such as a **brawdel** is needed to pierce a hole through the cotton moulds used for making berries.

Pins are used throughout this book for general sewing and for most of the stick and paste projects. **Glass-headed stainless steel pins** are a must for weaving and for using with PVA-treated ribbon while it dries. **Brass pins** are used for the fruit, sunflowers and bridesmaid's pomander as they are not removed and are more decorative.

Adhesives

Glue of some type is used in many of the projects. A **strong glue** that dries to a clear finish and is suitable for fabric and card is needed for several of the projects. Spray adhesive is useful for projects such as the dyed lampshades. It is applied evenly straight from the can and allows for repositioning. **PVA medium,** available from hardware stores, is used to make a solution that will stiffen ribbon.

Strip iron-on adhesive looks similar to interfacing but when ironed between two pieces of fabric turns to glue under the heat and fuses the fabric together. Take care not to coat the hot sole plate of your iron with glue by allowing it to touch the strip adhesive.

General

Use an **air-soluble vanishing marking pen** to mark fabric or ribbon. Marks made by these pens disappear within hours if exposed to daylight. In darker conditions it may take a few days.

A **transparent set square,** a long **transparent ruler** and a **tape measure** will be needed for most of the projects.

Dressmaker's carbon paper is used to transfer motifs straight onto fabric.

A **dressmaker's cutting board** is necessary for weaving ribbon as the ribbon ends need to be pinned to the work surface. If you do not have a cutting board, use layers of **corrugated cardboard** or a **cork mat** 10 cm (4 in) larger than the weaving you are working.

Clip fabric into an **embroidery hoop** to keep it smooth when working an embroidery. Make sure that the fabric is taut and stays in position by tightening the outer ring of the hoop.

Techniques

The same basic techniques occur in many of the projects. Before starting any project, take time to read the techniques shown here carefully and to practise the methods needed.

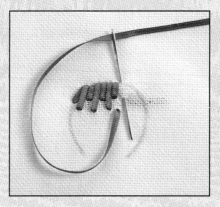

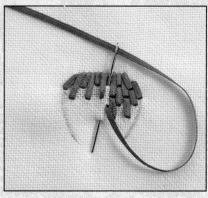

Long and Short Stitch 1 *In the first row the stitches are alternately long and short and closely follow the outline of the motif.*

2 *Continue working rows of equal length stitches to fill the area. Alter the length of the stitches at the side edges and when working the last row for a smooth outline.*

EMBROIDERY

Use 1.5 mm (¹/20 in) wide double satin ribbon only for ribbon embroidery, any wider will pucker as you work. To neaten, cut ribbon ends at the back of the work, leaving about 4 cm (1¹/2 in). Thread the ends through the back of the stitches already worked.

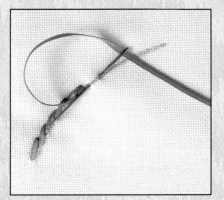

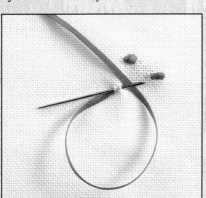

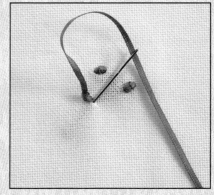

Stem Stitch 1 *Work from left to right. Insert the needle one stitch away through the right side of the fabric and bring up halfway along the side of the previous stitch.*

Bullion Knot 1 *Bring the needle up to the left of the mark. Take a small back stitch to the right of the stitch, bringing the needle point out where the ribbon emerges.*

2 *Wrap the ribbon three times around the needle. Holding the left thumb on the coiled ribbon, pull the needle through and insert where the ribbon originally emerged.*

Small Flower 1 *Bring the needle up at the top of a petal. Twist the ribbon and insert the needle at the centre of the flower. Repeat with the remaining petals.*

Large Flower 1 *Bring the needle up and insert again at the top of a petal. Bring up again at the bottom and pull the looped ribbon to the length of the petal.*

2 *Twist the loop and insert the needle through it. Take a small stitch over the loop and back through the fabric. Work a bullion knot in the centre of the petals.*

Rosebud or Bluebell 1 *Bring the needle out at the base of the flower motif. Take a slanting stitch to the right then to the left and work another 'V' inside the first.*

2 *Bring the needle out at the top of the flower and insert again at the base of the 'V'. Repeat, slightly slanting the stitches to the left and right of the central stitch.*

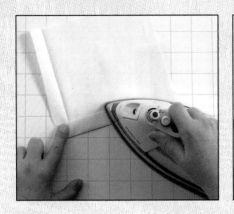

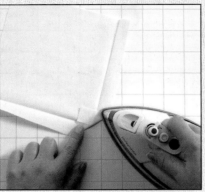

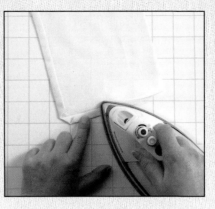

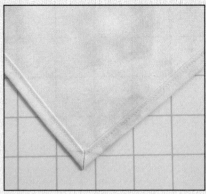

Mitred Corners

1 *Press a double hem to the wrong side along both edges, meeting at the corner.*

2 *Where the inner hem creases meet, press the corner to the wrong side at a 45 degree angle to the hem so that the crease on the right side follows exactly the same line as that on the wrong side.*

3 *Trim the corner to measure the finished width of the hem. Turn under the raw edges of the hem so that they run along the inside of the hem crease.*

4 *Stitch hem in place and press.*

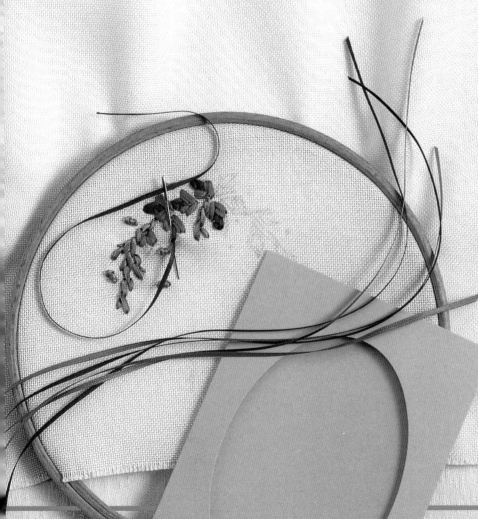

PVA-Treated Ribbon

1 *Using an egg cup as a measure and mixing two parts of water to eight of PVA medium, prepare the glue mix in a large basin. Stir well. Pass each length of ribbon through the glue mix, pushing it down into the liquid with a wooden stick or spoon.*

2 *Hold the treated ribbon over the basin and run the strip through your fingers to remove any excess glue. Wrap a piece of foil around a washing line or clothes airer for protection and hang the treated ribbon up in a warm room. Place layers of newspaper under the ribbon to catch any drips.*

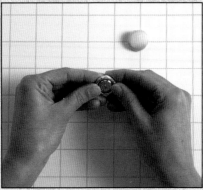

Covering a Button

1 *Use pinking shears to cut a circle from ribbon 1 cm (²/₅ in) larger all round than the button. Work running stitches around the edge of the circle. Do not cut off the thread. Place the button top side down onto the wrong side of the ribbon circle and pull the thread, gathering the circle edges around the button. Secure with few small stitches. Use the blunt edge of a scissor blade to push the gathered edge under the teeth around the button rim.*

2 *Press the back onto the button until it clips into place.*

Curling Method

1 *Place the item to be curled between the thumb of one hand and the blade of a pair of scissors. Draw the fabric or paper over the scissor blade. Repeat over the same area if more curl is needed.*

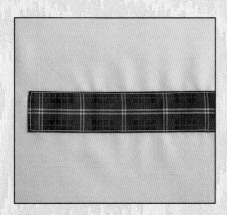

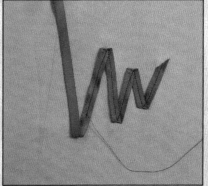

Stitching Wide Ribbon to Fabric

1 *Line up the edge of the ribbon along the positioning line. Machine stitch along one side of the ribbon close to one edge, then stitch along the other edge, working in the same direction as before.*

Outlining Method

1 *Stitching along the centre of the narrow ribbon, fold the ribbon to allow it to follow the curved line of the pattern. Cut the ribbon ends at angles to neaten before stitching in place.*

Covering a Sphere

1 *Cut the ribbon ends into a point. Pin one point to the sphere, then wrap the ribbon tightly around the ball, changing the angle slightly each round but making sure that the ribbon edges overlap. Tuck the remaining end underneath and use brass pins to pin in place.*

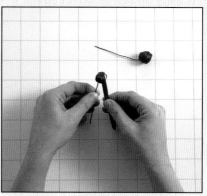

Grapes/Cherries/Berries

1 *Pierce a hole through the centre of the cotton mould using a sharp-pointed brawdel. Thread onto green wire and take a short end around the bead, tucking about 1 cm (²/5 in) of it into the hole where the longer end emerges. With your finger holding the wire in the hole, pull the longer end tightly to secure.*

2 *Cut the ends of the ribbon into points. Apply glue along the length of the ribbon and wrap around the mould, beginning close to the wire stem and changing the angle of the ribbon slightly each round. Take care to overlap the edges of the ribbon. Pin the remaining ribbon end in place, removing the pin when dry.*

Pineapple/Sunflower Centre

1 *Cut the wire-edged ribbon ends into points. Pin one end into the oasis and place your forefinger on the pinned ribbon point. Loop the ribbon over the finger and pin it into the oasis underneath the finger tip. Continue looping and pinning the ribbon until the oasis has been covered. Tuck the end into the bottom of a loop.*

2 *Scrunch the ribbon loops to look like squashed ribbon 'puffs', making sure that no oasis is visible and that you have covered all the pins.*

PVA-Treated Ribbon Flowers

Lily

1 *Wind the lower half of two 6 cm (2²/₅ in) pearl-headed flower stamens around the top of a 10cm (4 in) length of florist's stub wire.*

2 *Use the lily petal template on p. 99 to cut out five petals from 50 mm (2 in) wide cream double satin ribbon stiffened with PVA solution (see p. 13). Attaching one petal at a time and covering the twisted wires, curl the petals around the wire stem at the top, making sure that the petals overlap. Wind fine florist's wire around the base of each petal to fix in place.*

3 *Beginning at the base of the petals, cover the stem with green florist's paper tape. Slightly bend the stem. Holding the petals at the base, curl the petals away from the flower centre (see p. 14), taking care not to pull the petals away from their fixed position.*

Primrose and Anemonies

1 *The primrose and the anemone are made in the same way. Use the template on p. 99 to cut out primrose or anemone shapes from the ribbon specified, treating it first in PVA solution (see p. 13). Pierce a hole through the centre of the petals with a sharp-pointed thick sewing needle. Thread a 6 cm (2²/₅ in) long pearl-headed stamen through the hole.*

2 *Pinch the petals at the centre of the flower so that they surround the pearl head. Wrap green florist's paper tape several times tightly around the base of the petal shape to hold it tightly against the pearl. Continue wrapping florist's tape down the flower stem. Curl the petals (see p. 14).*

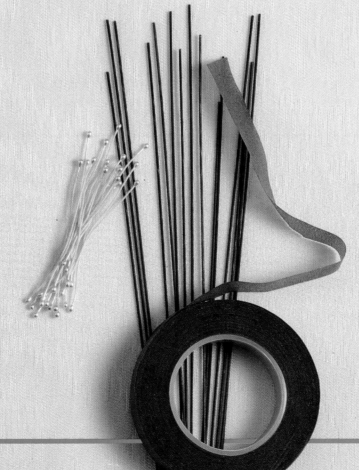

Bluebell

1 *Cut five small petals for each bluebell from ribbon treated with PVA solution (see p. 13). Keeping the pearl-heads of two stamens level with the top of the petals, attach the petals to the stem one at a time and cover the stem as for the lily.*

Gypsophila

1 *Using the template on p. 99 cut out five tiny flower shapes. Thread a 6 cm (2²/₅ in) long pearl-headed stamen through the centre of each flower. Pinch to curve the flower around the pearl head and cover the stems as for the primroses. Using green florist's paper tape, bind the five stems together at the base. Bend the top of each individual stem.*

Tight Rosebud with Stem

1 *Use ribbons with no right or wrong side. Cut the ribbon ends so that they are angled away from each other. Fold one end over so that the angled cut end is parallel to the straight long ribbon edge. Bend the top 1.5 cm (¹/₂ in) of a stub wire over the folded ribbon and pinch tight using pliers.*

2 *Roll the wire between your fingers towards the main length of ribbon. Once the point has been concealed, make a 45 degree fold to the back of the main length of ribbon so that it hangs downwards. Roll the ribbon tightly around the wire, keeping the lower edges level at the base of the rosebud and stopping at the point where the straight edges cross. Fold the ribbon again as before and continue to roll. Repeat until all the ribbon has been used.*

3 *Secure the ribbon around the wire with a few stitches through the lower edges of the rosebud. Wrap a 20 cm (8 in) length of fine wire tightly around the base of the rosebud and, using a pair of pliers, twist the ends tightly together. Wrap the twisted ends around the base of the rosebud.*

4 *Stretching the florist's tape to make it sticky, wrap it around the base of the rosebud, covering the fine wire and overlapping the edges. Spiral the tape around and down the stem of the rosebud, stretching it to make sure it adheres to itself properly.*

Loose Rosebud Without Stem

1 *Use ribbons with no right or wrong side. Cut the ribbon ends so that they are angled away from each other and fold one end over so that the cut end is parallel to the straight long ribbon edge. Fold the point back onto the main length of ribbon and stitch in place along the lower edge.*

2 *Begin rolling the ribbon into a tight bud, keeping the lower straight edge level. Stitch the lower edge to secure as you work. Fold the ribbon to the back of the work at a 45 degree angle and roll along the lower straight edge to the point where the straight edges cross. Fold again to the back of the work and roll along the new, lower straight edge. Repeat folding, rolling and stitching ribbon until the whole length has been used. Wrap a 30 cm (12 in) length of fine wire around the base of the rosebud, leaving 6 cm (2 1/2 in) ends for attaching.*

Square rose

1 *Cut the ribbon ends at angles to prevent fraying. Lay the ribbon vertically on a work surface and, about 10 cm (4 in) from the lower end, fold at a 45 degree angle to the right. Fold the ribbon towards you again at right angles, laying the long end parallel to the short end but leaving a small gap.*

2 *Holding the ribbon layers in place with one hand, continue to fold the ribbon at right angles to form a square with a small hole in the centre. Leave a 10 cm (4 in) end free.*

3 *Still holding the ribbon layers in place in one hand, push the remaining end through the centre hole of the folded square. Pull this end through to the back of the work and keep pulling gently until the top of the rose begins to twist around.*

4 *Trim the ends to about 1 cm (2/5 in) and stitch in place flat against the underside of the rose.*

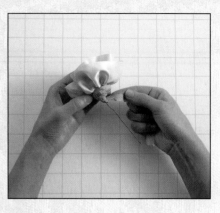

Peony

1 *Cut the ends of a 50 cm (20 in) length of 25 mm (1 in) double satin ribbon to angle away from each other. Work a line of running stitches about 5 mm (¹/₅ in) from the long edge and gather the ribbon up tightly. Secure the thread. Neaten the ends of a 1 m (1¹/₄ yd) length of 75 mm (3 in) wide double satin ribbon and gather up as for the narrower ribbon.*

2 *Roll up the gathered narrower ribbon, stitching the gathered edges together as you roll to secure. Roll the wider ribbon around the narrower one, stitching the wider ribbon to the rolled up narrower ribbon along the gathered edge, then to itself.*

3 *Wrap a 25 cm (10 in) length of stub wire 1 cm (²/₅ in) up around the gathered base of the peony. Twist the ends tightly together to pinch in the base of the flower. Bend the wire to the centre of the underside of the flower, then bend again to form the stalk. Stitch the stub wire in place along the gathered edges to prevent it slipping off the ribbon.*

4 *Stretching florist's tape to make it sticky, wrap it around the base of the peony to cover the stub wire. Overlapping the edges, spiral the tape around the base of the peony, folding the tape at right angles to itself as you spiral towards the stem. Wrap the tape around and down the length of the stem.*

Basic Double Gathered Rosette

1 *Using lengths of narrower and wider double satin ribbon, join the ribbon ends together with a 5 mm (¹/₅ in) seam in backstitch to form two separate rings. Press the seams open and trim to 3 mm (¹/₁₀ in). Turn the rings inside out, press the seam along the join, then work another 5 mm (¹/₅ in) seam in backstitch. Turn the rings right side out and press.*

2 *Place the wider ribbon ring inside the narrower ring and, matching the seams, work a line of running stitches close to one edge through both ribbon layers. Tightly gather up this edge and secure the gathering thread with a few tiny stitches.*

3 *Stitch the hole in the centre of the rosette closed by taking stitches across the centre and drawing them up. Finish the rosette with the central trim recommended in the project instructions.*

For a single gathered rosette use only one ribbon ring.

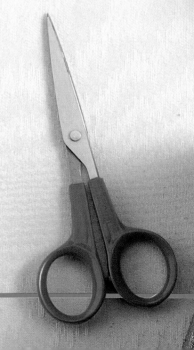

Double-Layered Pleated Rosette

1 *Cut equal lengths of narrower and wider ribbon. Line up the long edges of the two lengths and, with the narrower ribbon on the outside, join the ends taking a 5 mm (¹/₅ in) seam in backstitch to form a ring. Press the seam open and trim to half its width. Turn the ring inside out and sew another 5 mm (¹/₅ in) seam in backstitch. Press the seam and turn the ring right side out.*

2 *Work a line of small running stitches close to the edges through the two layers of ribbon. Fasten off the thread securely without gathering the ribbon edge.*

3 *Pin the ribbon layers together in pleats around the inner edge, taking about 2 cm (³/₄ in) for each pleat and allowing each one enough fullness to grade out to form a circle. Steam press and remove pins.*

4 *Secure the pleats by stitching them together around the inner edge. Take several stitches across the centre of the rosette and draw up to close the hole. Rearrange the outer edge of the pleats once more and press. Refer to the project instructions for the specific decoration to be sewn over the centre of the rosette.*

Use the same method for a single-layered rosette, using one length of ribbon only.

Single-looped basic bow with single or double tails

1 *Overlapping the ends by 2 cm (³/4 in), join the ribbon lengths intended for the bow loops to form a ring and work a few stitches through both ribbon ends to hold them together where they meet. Flatten the ribbon ring with the ends centred and without creasing the loops. Secure in place with a few stitches.*

2 *Fold the tail in half to find the centre point. With right sides face upwards, centre the flattened bow loops over the tails and sew in place, taking a few stitches over the previous ones. If the instructions require, add another layer of bow tails right side up directly below the first.*

Double-looped bow with single tails

1 *Make up two bow loops as for the single-looped basic bow. Insert the needle into the centre of both flattened bow loops, twist bow loops to form a cross and stitch through all layers.*

2 *Fold the tail length in half to find the centre point. With right sides face upwards, centre the double bow loop cross over the tails and stitch through all layers at the central point. Pleat the ribbon for the bow knot to measure 2 cm (³/4 in) and wrap around the centre of the bow, stitching at the back of the bow to secure as for the single-looped basic bow.*

3 *Pleat the ribbon for the bow knot once along its length to about 2 cm (³/4 in) wide. Starting at the back of the bow under the tails, wrap the bow knot ribbon several times around the centre of the bow, so gathering in the bow at the centre. Trim the knot end at the back of the bow and stitch the end in place. Neaten the ribbon ends as required in the instructions.*

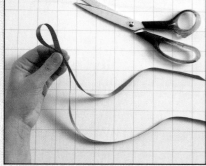

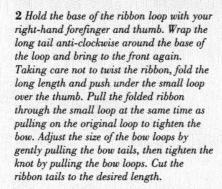

Tied Bow

1 *Fold the ribbon length in half to find the centre. Hold the ribbon between the left-hand thumb and forefinger at this point. Depending on the ultimate size of the bow you wish to make, loop up some of the ribbon length above the thumb and to the back of the work.*

2 *Hold the base of the ribbon loop with your right-hand forefinger and thumb. Wrap the long tail anti-clockwise around the base of the loop and bring to the front again. Taking care not to twist the ribbon, fold the long length and push under the small loop over the thumb. Pull the folded ribbon through the small loop at the same time as pulling on the original loop to tighten the bow. Adjust the size of the bow loops by gently pulling the bow tails, then tighten the knot by pulling the bow loops. Cut the ribbon tails to the desired length.*

Soft Furnishings

Explore the possibilities of unusual ribbon techniques such as weaving, ruching, embroidery and appliqué to bring new dimensions of texture and colour to your furnishing scheme.

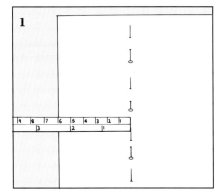

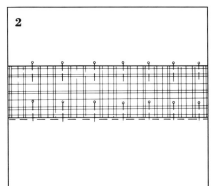

1 *From a 132 x 192 cm (52 x 76 in) length of heavyweight yellow cotton furnishing fabric cut a 112 x 112 cm (44 x 44 in) square. Press and lay flat. The ribbon is stitched onto the fabric in the position and order set out in the chart on p. 106. To place the first ribbon, position a line of pins on the right side of the fabric 6 cm (2²/₅ in) from and parallel with one edge.*

2 *With the straight-cut ribbon end to the fabric edge, place the 75 mm (3 in) wide tartan ribbon with its long edge just inside the pinned line. Pin, then machine in place with a straight stitch (see p. 14). Dry press on the wrong side of the work. Following the chart on p. 106, sew on the ribbons one at a time, marking the position before pinning and stitching in place. Dry press after stitching each ribbon.*

◀ *To make the throw you will need: 3.5 m (4 yd) of 75 mm (3 in) wide tartan polyester ribbon, 4.5 m (5 yd) of 38 mm (1½ in) wide tartan polyester ribbon, 1.5 m (1¾ yd) of 50 mm (2 in) wide rust velvet ribbon, 2.5 m (2¾ yd) of 50 mm (2 in) wide green velvet ribbon, 3.5 m (4 yd) of 20 mm (¾ in) wide rust velvet ribbon and 2 m (2¼ yd) of 20 mm (¾ in) wide green velvet ribbon.*

▼ *Traditional tartan and rich velvet ribbons on heavy cotton fabric make a luxurious throw to enhance any furnishing scheme. Take care to choose a colour that matches the tartan and shows off the texture of the velvet.*

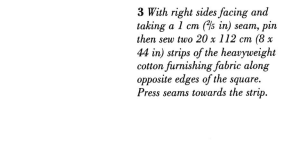

3 With right sides facing and taking a 1 cm (²/₅ in) seam, pin then sew two 20 x 112 cm (8 x 44 in) strips of the heavyweight cotton furnishing fabric along opposite edges of the square. Press seams towards the strip.

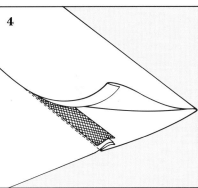

4 Press a 1 cm (²/₅ in) hem to the wrong side along the long edge of the attached strips. Lay a length of strip iron-on adhesive just above the pressed seam, then fold the strip in half with wrong sides together and with the folded edge just covering the seam stitching. Steam press in place. Machine stitch the hem in place from the right side, working close to the seam.

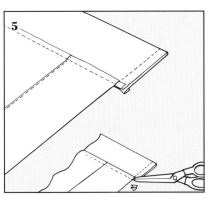

5 With 1 cm (²/₅ in) overhang at each end and taking a 1 cm (²/₅ in) seam, stitch two 20 x 132 cm (8 x 52 in) strips of the furnishing fabric along the remaining two edges of the square. Press seams towards the strip, then press a 1 cm (²/₅ in) hem to the wrong side along the long edges of the strips. Fold the strip in half with right sides together and with the folded hem edge just covering the seam. Stitch ends at right-angles to the fold, taking a 1 cm (²/₅ in) seam. Snip corners.

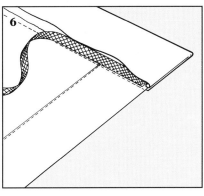

6 Pushing out the corners carefully, turn the borders right side out. Place a length of strip iron-on adhesive along the seam, just covering the stitching. Position the border hem over the strip and steam press in place. Machine stitch the hem from the right side as before.

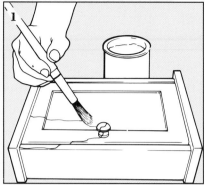

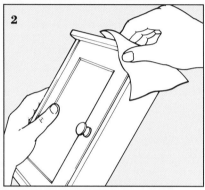

1 *You will need a plain key cabinet with a door panel 10 x 18 cm (4 x 7 in). Sand the surface of the cabinet inside and out and paint in blue. Leave to dry. Apply another coat of paint in pale green. Leave to dry. Repeat the last two coats of paint once more, then finish by giving the cabinet two final coats of blue paint.*

2 *When the paint has completely dried, rub the surface with finegrade glasspaper to remove the paint layers - pay particular attention to corners, edges and the handle - leaving the surface smooth when you have finished.*

◀ *Keep your keys safely in one place and add vibrant colour to your hallway with this key cabinet and its bold geometric panel, inspired by the brilliant Aztec textiles from South America.*

▼ *Tie oddments of the embroidery ribbons to the keys for a burst of colour when you open the door!*

3 *Cut a 10 x 18 cm (4 x 7 in) piece of plastic canvas with a ratio of five holes to 2 cm (¾ in). Refer to the chart on p. 97 for ribbon colours, lengths and widths. Working from the chart, thread a tapestry needle with a length of black double satin ribbon. Leave about 10 cm (4 in) of ribbon at the back of the canvas and bring the needle up through the edge hole two rows down. Keeping the ribbon flat, take it over the canvas edge and bring the needle up through the next hole along. Continue to work in this way to the end of the row. Thread the needle and ribbon through the back of a few stitches and trim.*

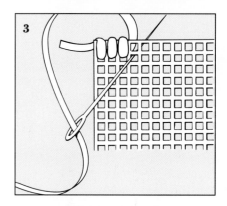

4 *Continue stitching the colour blocks using lengths of fuschia, jade, turquoise, red and orange ribbon. Leave about 10 cm (4 in) of ribbon at the back of the canvas and bring the needle up through the same starting hole as for the black ribbon. Follow the chart by inserting the needle two holes further down. It is important to keep the ribbon flat so the stitches cover the canvas. Complete the embroidery, working the stitches to the length indicated on the chart.*

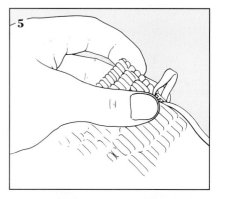

5 *To neaten the sides of the canvas, oversew with the black ribbon along the edges, working into each edge hole.*

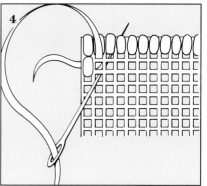

6 *Making sure the back of the embroidery is even, smear the back and the door panel with adhesive. Leave until slightly tacky then press the embroidery firmly in place. If necessary, weigh the canvas down with a heavy object while it is drying.*

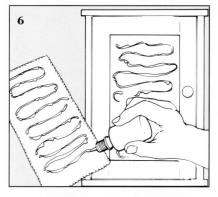

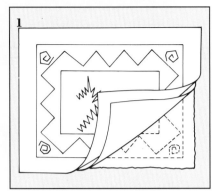

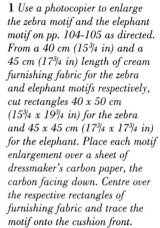

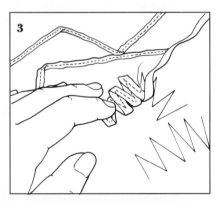

1 *Use a photocopier to enlarge the zebra motif and the elephant motif on pp. 104-105 as directed. From a 40 cm (15¾ in) and a 45 cm (17¾ in) length of cream furnishing fabric for the zebra and elephant motifs respectively, cut rectangles 40 x 50 cm (15¾ x 19¾ in) for the zebra and 45 x 45 cm (17¾ x 17¾ in) for the elephant. Place each motif enlargement over a sheet of dressmaker's carbon paper, the carbon facing down. Centre over the respective rectangles of furnishing fabric and trace the motif onto the cushion front.*

2 *Cut a piece of mediumweight iron-on interfacing 50 x 40 cm (20 x 15¾ in) for the zebra cushion and 45 x 45 cm (17¾ x 17¾ in) for the elephant cushion. Iron onto the wrong side of the cushion front.*

3 *You will need 4.5 m (5 yd) of black and 2.5 m (2¾ yd) of terracotta single satin ribbon 7 mm (¼ in) wide for the zebra cushion, and 3.5 m (4 yd) of aubergine and 5 m (5½ yd) of gold single satin ribbon 7 mm (¼ in) wide for the elephant cushion. Snip one ribbon end at an angle. Lay the ribbon over the beginning of a straight stretch in the motif and stitch over the motif using the ribbon outlining method (see p. 14). Stitch to within a few centimetres of the end of the motif. Trim the ribbon end at an angle and stitch down, overlapping with the starting point if the pattern is continuous.*

4 *For the back, cut two pieces of cream cotton furnishing fabric 27.5 x 40 cm (10¾ x 15¾ in) and 29.5 x 40 cm (11½ x 15¾ in) for the zebra cushion, and 25 x 45 cm (9⅞ x 18 in) and 27 x 45 cm (10⅝ x 18 in) for the elephant cushion. Press a 3 cm (1¼ in) hem to the wrong side along one long edge of the wider back half and 1 cm (⅖ in) along one long edge of the other back half. Neaten both with a zigzag stitch. Using a straight stitch close to the fold, sew the narrow hem in place.*

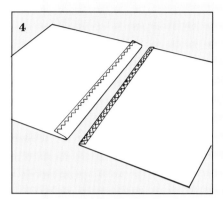

5 *For the fastening, cut a 30 cm (12 in) strip of 2 cm (¾ in) wide adhesive-backed Velcro. Stitch one half of the Velcro strip in the centre of the wider hem. Stick Velcro strips together, peel off adhesive backing. Overlap the two neatened back edges by 3 cm (1⅕ in), peel the Velcro apart and stitch the remaining strip in place.*

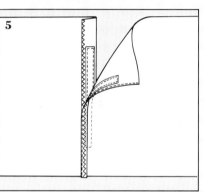

6 *Fasten the two back cushion pieces together with the Velcro. With the right side uppermost, stitch close to the edge down the fold of the hem as far as the Velcro. Stitch across the end of the Velcro for 2.5 cm (1 in). Turn and stitch back up the work. Do this at both ends of the fastening. With right sides facing, stitch back and front together taking a 1 cm (⅖ in) seam. Snip corners and turn right side out through the opening. Press, then insert cushion pad.*

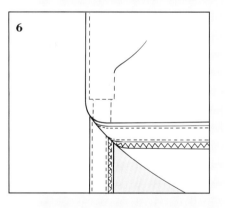

◀ *Unusual cushions reflecting the earthy colours of the African plain are quick and easy to make using the ribbon outlining method and our basic cushion-cover pattern. Team them with natural fabrics and ethnic accessories to create a warm and colourful furnishing scheme.*

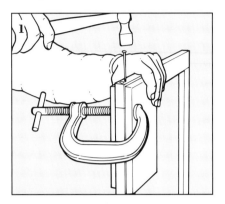

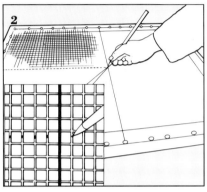

1 *Cut a 2 x 4 x 242 cm (³⁄₄ x 1³⁄₅ x 95 in) length of wood into two 57 cm (22¹⁄₂ in) and two 64 cm (25 in) lengths. Lay the two longer lengths horizontally 57 cm (22¹⁄₂ in) apart, then place the shorter two vertically each end. Place each corner between two pieces of wood and grip with a 'G clamp'. Drill two holes 2 cm (³⁄₄ in) apart through the side of one piece of wood into the end of the other. Hammer 7.5 cm (3 in) grip nails into these holes. The finished frame should measure 57 x 72 cm (22¹⁄₂ x 28³⁄₈ in).*

2 *Stick carpet tape over the cut edges of a piece of 55 x 71 cm (21⁵⁄₈ x 28 in) rug canvas with seven holes per 5 cm (2 in). Pull the canvas tightly over the frame and securely pin to the wood with drawing pins. Use a felt-tipped pen to mark the centre warp thread and the centre line of holes from selvedge to selvedge.*

3 *Refer to the chart and key on p. 96 to work the wallhanging. You will need 20 m (22 yd) of jade, 40 m (44 yd) of airforce blue, 18 m (20 yd) of chocolate, 23 m (25¼ yd) of terracotta and 14 m (15½ yd) of ochre single satin ribbon, all 36 mm (1½ in) wide, and 9 m (10 yd) of 38 mm (1½ in) wide bronze lurex ribbon. Begin by working the centre two stitches on the chart at the point where the drawn lines meet. Leaving the end of each ribbon length free at the back of the canvas, work each stitch vertically over two weft threads and stitch over the loose ends at the back as you go. Complete the pattern working from the chart.*

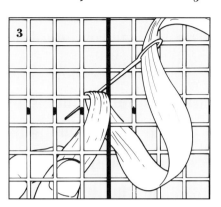

4 *Remove the work from the frame. Lightly steam the embroidered canvas on the wrong side without bringing the iron into contact with the ribbon. Gently pull the canvas into shape. Trim the canvas edges to within 3 cm (1½ in) of the outer stitches and fold to the back. Slip stitch in place so that the canvas does not show around the edges of the work from the right side.*

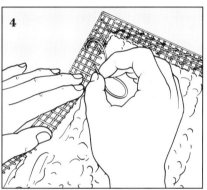

5 *Cut 2.38 m (2 yd 22 in) of 36 mm (1½ in) wide chocolate single satin ribbon into 14 17 cm (6½ in) lengths. Fold each length in half widthways with wrong sides together and centre over each terracotta section along the long edges of the canvas. Stitch 4 cm (1½ in) of the loops' cut ends to the folded edge and back of the canvas.*

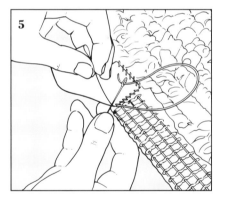

6 *With wrong sides facing, slip stitch 2.25 m (2 yd 17 in) of 36 mm (1½ in) wide chocolate single satin ribbon along all four folded outer edges of the canvas. Folding the ribbon at the corners to fit, stitch the inner edges of the ribbon in place. Slip two 70 cm (27½ in) long dowels 2 cm (¾ in) in diameter through the top and bottom loops.*

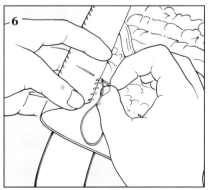

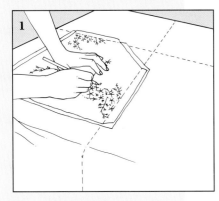

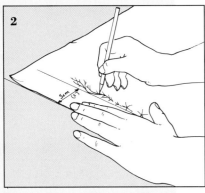

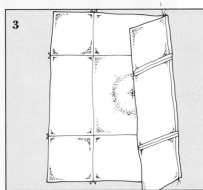

1 *From a 1.4 x 5 m (55 in x 5½ yd) length of evenweave linen with 27 threads per 2.5 cm (1 in) cut a square 122 x 122 cm (48 x 48 in) and fold into quarters. Stitch running stitches along the folds. Using dressmaker's carbon paper, transfer charts A and B on pp. 108-109 onto this central panel, lining up the dotted lines on the charts with the running stitches and transferring chart B onto each quarter section of the fabric. Embroider the central panel referring to the key on p. 108 for ribbon specifications and to the embroidery steps on p. 12.*

2 *Transfer chart C on p. 108 onto each corner of the central panel, positioning the dotted lines 5 cm (2 in) from the edges, and onto two diagonally opposite corners on each of four 67 x 67 cm (26½ x 26½ in) corner squares cut from the same fabric. Embroider the motifs. Positioning the dotted lines on Chart D on p. 108 5 cm (2 in) from the edges, transfer the motif onto the remaining corners of the corner squares and onto each corner of four 122 x 67 cm (48 x 26½ in) side panels cut from the evenweave linen. Embroider the motifs.*

3 *With right sides together and taking 1.5 cm (³/5 in) seams, sew one side panel to opposite sides of the central panel. Join the corner squares to each end of the remaining side panels, checking that the motifs on the corner squares mirror each other. Press seams open. Matching the seams, join the side strips to each side of the centre strip so that there is a large corner motif on each outer corner of the bedspread. Press seams open.*

4 *Using a vanishing marking pen, draw a line on the right side of the fabric 7 mm (³/₁₀ in) one side of each seam. Using 10.12 m (11 yd 4 in) of 15 mm (³/₅ in) wide white garland jacquard ribbon, align 2.53 m (2 yd 28 in) lengths along the drawn lines over each seam and stitch along both edges.*

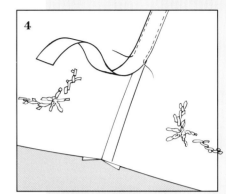

5 *Mitring the corners (see p. 13), turn 14 mm (¹/₂ in) over to the wrong side to form a double hem all around the bedspread. Machine stitch hem in place about 5 mm (¹/₅ in) from the hem edge. Press.*

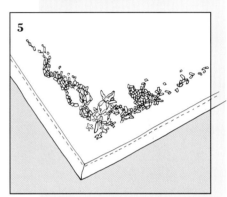

6 *Cut 160 cm (32 in) of 3 mm (¹/₁₀ in) wide white double satin ribbon into six equal lengths and tie six tied bows (see p. 23). Sew the tied bows to the ends of the jacquard ribbon over the hem stitching.*

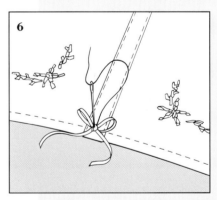

◀ *An embroidered bedspread will not only add a personal touch to your bedroom but will one day become a family heirloom. Alternatively, you could show it off by draping it as a wallhanging.*

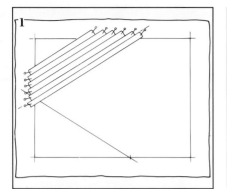

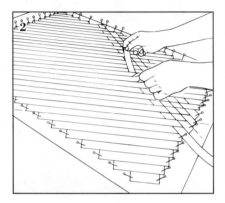

1 *Draw a 47 x 64 cm (18$\frac{1}{2}$ x 25$\frac{1}{2}$ in) rectangle on brown paper, positioning the shorter edges top and bottom. Mark the centre of the lower short side and 39 cm (15$\frac{2}{5}$ in) up each long side. Draw diagonal lines through these points. Pin to a cutting board. Using 10.5 m (11$\frac{1}{4}$ yd) of 22 mm (4/5 in) wide velvet ribbon in each of purple, wine, gold and moss and, with ribbons right side down, line up the gold ribbon along the left-hand diagonal line. Pin ribbon outside the rectangle and trim 1 cm (2/5 in) from the pins. Pin alternating lengths of gold and purple ribbon to cover the rectangle.*

2 *Following the right-hand diagonal line, weave the wine ribbon under the gold and over the purple lengths. Continue covering the rectangle with alternate lengths of wine and moss ribbon, weaving the moss over the gold and under the purple ribbon lengths.*

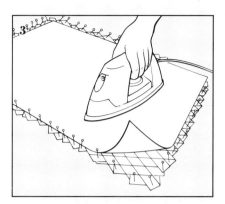

3 *Steam press 47 x 64 cm (18¹/₂ x 25¹/₂ in) of iron-on interfacing onto the centre of the weaving. Remove the pins. Trim the ribbon ends level with the edge of the interfacing. Sew the ribbon ends in place by stitching all around the weaving 1 cm (²/₅ in) from the edge.*

4 *With right sides facing, bring the two shorter ends of the weaving together. Taking a 1.5 cm (³/₅ in) seam, stitch, leaving a 30 cm (12 in) gap in the centre of the seam. Press seam open. Insert a 30 cm (12 in) zip into the seam opening, pin, tack and stitch in place. Turn the woven tube inside out.*

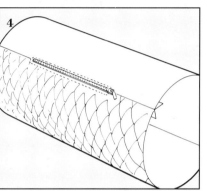

5 *Join the shorter ends of two 12 x 63 cm (4³/₄ x 24⁴/₅ in) dark green velvet strips with a 1.5 cm (³/₅ in) seam to form two rings. Press seams open. Sew a velvet ring to each end of the woven tube, taking a 1 cm (²/₅ in) seam. Press seams towards the weaving. With the woven tube inside out, insert a 61 cm (24 in) round cushion pad 45 cm (17³/₄ in) long. Leaving the zip open, gather up the raw edges of the velvet fabric at the centre of the pad ends and pin in place. Stitch through the gathers to secure. Remove the pins and cushion pad. Turn the cushion cover right side out and insert the cushion pad.*

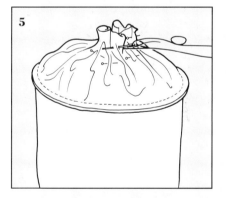

6 *Make two plaits from 32 cm (16¹/₂ in) lengths of wine, moss and purple ribbon. Cut the remaining ribbon into lengths 15-25 cm (6-10 in), then divide into two equal bunches. Stitch the ribbon lengths together 1 cm (²/₅ in) from the ends. Stitch to the beginning of the plaits. Allowing the loose ribbons to hang down and curling the plait around the stitched ends, sew to the centre of each gathered end, tucking the plait end underneath itself to neaten. Cut the trailing ribbon ends at angles.*

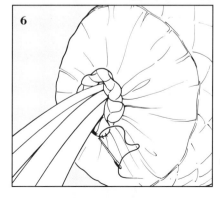

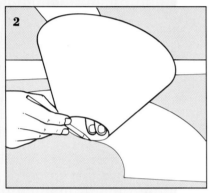

1 *Make up purple and jade fabric paint. Use cold water to dampen a 25 cm (10 in) long skein of 2.5 m (2¾ yd) of white 5 mm (⅕ in) wide double satin ribbon for the large flower motif or 10 m (11 yd) of white 3 mm (¹⁄₁₀ in) wide double satin ribbon for the allover pattern. Lay the skein on kitchen paper towels. Either paint the ribbon in a single colour, applying more thickly in some areas than in others and adding touches of contrasting colour, or paint bands of colour across the skein, allowing the colours to run into each other. Dry the ribbon with a hairdryer.*

2 *With a pencil, mark the shape of a lampshade 25 cm (10 in) in diameter on white paper, beginning with a straight line for the back seam and marking along the top and bottom edges of the shade as you roll it. Cut out the resulting paper shape.*

3 *Matching edges, fold the paper shape in half to mark the centre front. Wrap the paper shape around the shade and secure with masking tape. Sketch in pencil a four petal flower on the front of the shade, using the foldline to keep it symmetrical. Draw lines curving and looping from the flower centre in each direction around the shade, meeting at the back. For the allover pattern, alternate four petal flowers with loops in rows, leaving 4 cm (1½ in) straight lines either side of the back edges.*

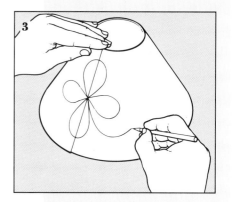

4 *Using dressmaker's carbon paper, transfer the motif pattern onto the right side of a 40 x 60 cm (15¾ x 23⅗ in) rectangle of plain mediumweight fabric. Allowing 1.5 cm (⅗ in) extra all round, draw around the fabric lampshade shape then cut out. Beginning and ending at the straight back edges, sew the ribbon onto the fabric along the motif outlines using the outlining method on p. 14. Fold 1 cm (⅖ in) along one straight edge to the wrong side. Press the work on the wrong side.*

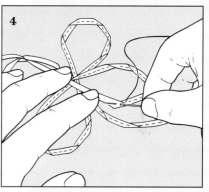

5 *Lay the fabric right side down on a flat protected work surface and spray liberally with spray adhesive. Smoothing out any bubbles, stick the fabric around the lampshade leaving 1.5 cm (⅗ in) overlap at the top and bottom of the frame and overlapping the folded straight edge at the back. Fold the fabric over the lower edge of the frame and stick to the inside. Snipping the fabric to fit, fold the top edge of the fabric to the inside of the shade and stick in place.*

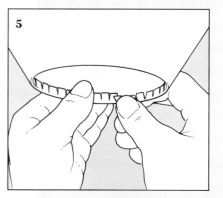

6 *Using strong clear glue, stick bias binding over the raw fabric edges inside the shade, stretching it to fit smoothly and overlapping the ends where they meet.*

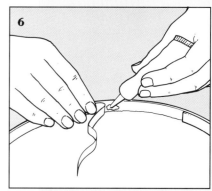

Soft Furnishings

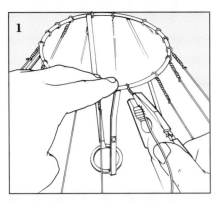

1 *For the woven lampshade you will need a coolie lampshade frame with three struts and measuring 33 cm (13 in) in diameter. Bend about 3 cm (1¼ in) of a length of florist's stub wire over the top ring of the shade and, using pliers, twist the ends together securely. Attach six wires between each strut.*

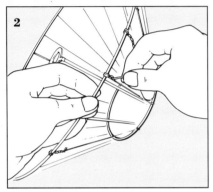

2 *Keeping the wire taut, bend the end of each wire over the lower ring and twist around itself to secure. Space the wires evenly between the struts.*

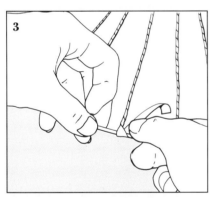

3 *Tightly wrap white floral tape around the top ring and the top of the struts. Continue to wrap the tape down the struts to the base. Cut the tape and wrap the end tightly in place.*

▶ *The sumptuous texture of folded tartan ribbon woven through a lampshade frame shows another exciting dimension of the possibilities of ribbon weaving.*

4 *You will need 18 m (20 yd) of 38 mm (1½ in) wide tartan ribbon for weaving the lampshade. Beginning at the top of the shade, loop approximately 16 cm (6 in) at the end of the ribbon around a main strut with the ribbon end on the inside of the shade. Fold the main length of ribbon in half widthways, enclosing the ribbon end within the inside of the fold. Secure the fold by neatly stitching through all four layers of ribbon. Weave the ribbon through the struts, spiralling downwards and ruching the ribbon as you go. When the struts have been covered, trim the ribbon end to 8 cm (3 in) and loop inwards around a strut, folding the main ribbon widthways round the cut end and stitching through all the layers.*

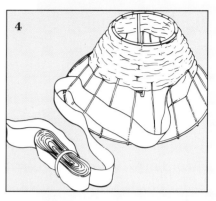

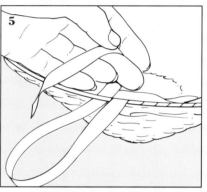

5 *Gluing the ends in place, wrap the upper and lower shade rings with 12 mm (½ in) wide single satin ribbon. This will take about 2.5 m (2¾ yd) of ribbon.*

1 *For the bowl of peonies, make a selection of purple, pink and red peonies as described on p. 20. Pack the bowl with dry oasis and arrange the peonies so that they fill the bowl.*

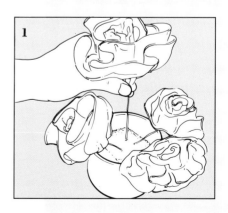

◀ *Add a bowl of brightly-coloured peonies as a contrast to the mottled effect of the black and white tartan ribbon.*

Table Decorations

Ribbons do not have to be tied in bows to create attractive table settings and displays! With the variety of ribbons available every kind of atmosphere can be achieved, from the elegance of an embroidered tablecloth made of linen and sheer ribbon to the Mediterranean feel of a burst of satin-petalled sunflowers. Use ribbons to garland your table on feast days and to provide decoration in your home all year round.

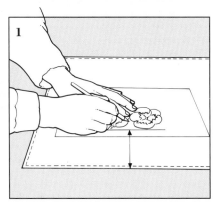

1 *Cut four 49.5 cm (19½ in) squares of embroidery linen with 27 threads per 2.5 cm (1 in). Mitring the corners (see p. 13), machine stitch double hems turning under 10 mm (⅖in) around each square. Use dressmaker's carbon paper to transfer the pansy motif on p. 107 onto each square, positioning the motif at 'A' towards one corner and the straight guidelines 12 cm (4¾ in) from the fabric edges.*

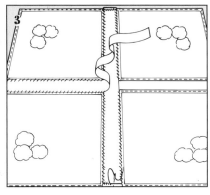

2 *To embroider the motifs use 1.5 mm (³⁄₅ in) wide double satin ribbon in willow (150 cm (60 in)), in pale blue (45 m (50 yd)), and in mid blue (23 m (25¼ yd)). Using an embroidery hoop, embroider the pansy motifs with long and short stitch (see p. 12), following the key on p. 107.*

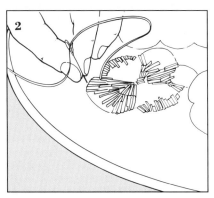

3 *Cut two 105 cm (41½ in) lengths of 56 mm (2⅕ in) wide white sheer ribbon. Stitch a narrow double hem at one end of each length. Place the four squares about 5 cm (2 in) apart, right sides down, in a square, positioning the motifs at the outer corners. Lay one ribbon length face down between the squares, keeping all hems level. Slip stitch the ribbon edges to the machine stitches of the adjoining squares. Repeat with the second length laid across the first. Neaten both ribbon ends with a narrow hem.*

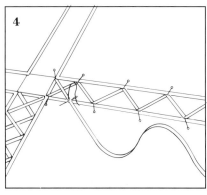

4 *On the right side mark points with a vanishing marking pen 5 cm (2 in) apart along the inner edges of the squares, ending 2.5 cm (1 in) from the outer edges. From 21.2 m (23¼ yd) of 7 mm (¼ in) wide white double satin ribbon cut four 150 cm (59 in) lengths. Pin the centre 5 cm (2 in) of each length between the inner fabric corners. Stitch in place. Form a lattice pattern by folding each ribbon end back and forth across the sheer ribbon and stitching in place at the marked points.*

5 *Cross the double satin ribbon ends so that they meet in the middle of the sheer ribbon hem edge. Fold the ends over to the wrong side of the work, forming narrow double hems and stitching in place so that they are invisible from the right side.*

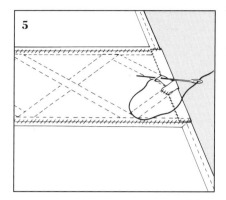

6 *Following the plan on p. 105, draw lines with a vanishing marking pen on each embroidered square. Working along the outside of the lines, use the outlining method (see p. 14) to stitch 150 cm (59 in) of 3 mm (¹/₁₀ in) wide mid blue double satin ribbon along line 'A' and 160 cm (63 in) of the same ribbon along line 'B'. Sewing along both edges, machine stitch 135 cm (54 in) of the 7 mm (¹/₄ in) wide white double satin ribbon along line 'C'. Trim ribbon ends within the hem area.*

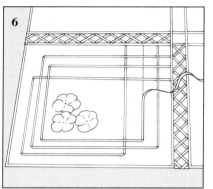

7 *Using the vanishing marking pen, mark points 5 cm (2 in) apart along the edges of the tablecloth, starting at the corners. Mark points 7 cm (2³/₄ in) apart along 6 m (6³/₄ yd) of the 7 mm (¹/₄ in) wide white double satin ribbon. Starting at one corner, take the ribbon away from the work, fold at the first mark and match the next mark on the ribbon with the next on the hem edge. Stitch the ribbon in place at the hem edge. Continue folding and stitching the ribbon where marked. Stitch the ribbon diagonally across the corners and continue folding. Press the folded ribbon. Turn under the remaining ribbon ends, overlap and stitch.*

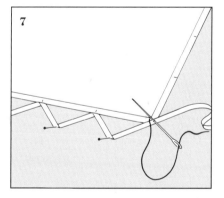

8 *Stitching along both edges of the 7 mm (¹/₄ in) wide double satin ribbon, sew 3.8 m (4 yd 5¹/₂ in) along the inner edges of each embroidered square. Stitch a 4.05 m (4¹/₂ yd) length around the outer edges of the tablecloth, covering the sheer ribbon hems. Stitch the ribbon end over the ribbon beginning, turning under 2 cm (1 in) to a double hem and matching the edges.*

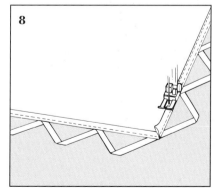

◀ *Recreate the elegance and delicacy of a bygone era with a beautiful tablecloth made from fine linen and satin and sheer ribbons. The exquisite embroidery can be achieved by anyone using narrow ribbon sewn in long and short stitch.*

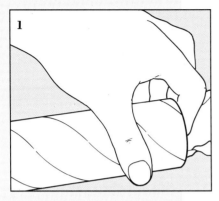

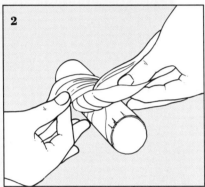

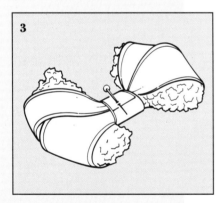

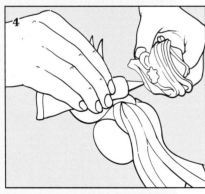

1 *To make the basic napkin ring, smoothly wrap a kitchen towel card tube in a sheet of polythene cut from a thick carrier bag, tucking the ends neatly into the centre of the tube. Secure with adhesive tape. Cut varying lengths of single satin ribbon of widths ranging from 40 mm (1½ in) to 60 mm (2⅖ in). Treat each ribbon length (not including the ribbon for the bow and rose) in a solution of PVA medium and water (see p. 13). Place on a protected work surface.*

2 *Starting with the thinnest ribbon and placing the pattern or satin side down, lay the ribbons on top of each other with the widest ribbon last. Smooth out any bubbles. Place the covered card tube across the middle of the ribbons at a right angle and bring the ends up around the tube and twist together. Place on a second polythene sheet, arrange the ends and check for bubbles and drips. Leave in a warm room until dry, then gently squeeze the card tube to remove from the napkin ring.*

3 *For the bow trim, cut 70 cm (2¾ in) of 39 mm (1½ in) wide single satin ribbon into one 10 cm (4 in) length for the knot and two 30 cm (12 in) lengths for the loops. Treat with PVA solution as before. Fold to form a fake double bow without tails (see p. 22), pinning the 'knot' end in place at the back of the bow. Arrange the bow then scrunch up silver foil into balls and stuff into the bow loops. Leave the bow to dry then remove the pins and foil.*

4 *Applying clear adhesive to the underside of the bow, stick to the napkin ring pressing firmly in place. For the rose trim, make a square rose using 2 m (2¼ yd) of 39 mm (1½ in) wide double satin ribbon (see p. 19) and attach to the napkin ring as for the bow.*

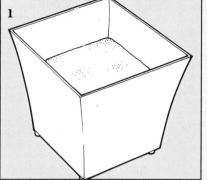

1 *Cut an oasis to fit into the base of your container.*

2 *Using 50 cm (20 in) of 38 mm (1½ in) wide ribbon per rosebud, make tight rosebuds with stems (see p. 18), covering only the base of the bud with florist's tape. Insert the stems into the oasis forming a 'dome' shape with the buds. Pack the container by carefully pulling the rosebuds apart to cram in extra roses.*

◀ *Masses of rosebuds made with matt ribbon would look as appealing if packed into a small basket or a terracotta flower pot.*

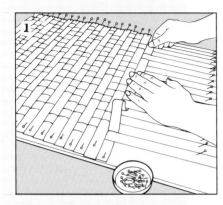

1 *Refer to the chart on p. 96 for ribbon colour, widths and lengths. With right sides down, lay 17 106 cm (41¾ in) lengths of charcoal ribbon side by side on a cutting board to form the warp ribbons, butting the long edges up against each other. Pin the first 60 cm (24 in) of warp ribbons in place. Cut 40 cm (16 in) lengths of each of the aubergine, terracotta and moss and, with right sides face downwards, weave the length through the charcoal warp ribbons from left to right according to the chart on p. 96. Pin each weft ribbon in place after weaving. Repeat the sequence shown on the chart along the 60 cm (24 in) of warp ribbons pinned in place.*

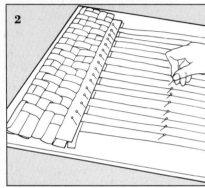

2 *Press a 40 x 60 cm (16 x 23½ in) square of mediumweight iron-on interfacing onto the wrong side of the weaving and remove the pins when cool. Roll up the weaving. Pin the remaining loose ends of warp ribbons in place at each end, butting up the long edges. Continue to weave along the length of the warp ribbons. Overlapping the interfacing by 1 cm (½ in), press a 40 x 47 cm (16 x 18½ in) square of iron-on interfacing onto the newly woven work and allow to cool.*

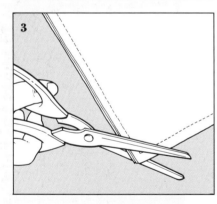

3 *Stitch around the weaving close to the edges of the work. Trim weaving to 1 cm (½ in) from the stitching so that the work measures 38 x 97 cm (15 x 38¼ in) edge to edge. With right sides together, stitch a 38 x 97cm (15 x 38¼ in) square of lining fabric to the weaving using a 1 cm (½ in) seam and leaving a 20 cm (8 in) gap in the seam. Snip the corners.*

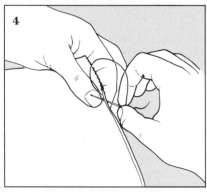

4 *Turn the work right side out, carefully pushing out the corners with the points of your scissors. Press the work carefully. Slip stitch the gap in the seam closed.*

Lengths of ribbon given here are for two bands of colour, charcoal and lupin, around a 25 cm (9¾ in) diameter bowl 18 cm (7½ in) deep.

1 *Paint a thin coat of undiluted PVA medium over a wire bowl with an even number of spokes. Leave to dry. Starting at the bowl base, weave an approximate length of 9 m (10 yd) of 36 mm (1⅖ in) wide ribbon through the first row of base spokes leaving free 8 cm (3 in) at the beginning. Weave the free end back along the ribbon and pinch the two layers of ribbon in half, enclosing the cut end of the ribbon. Neatly stitch through all four layers at the edges.*

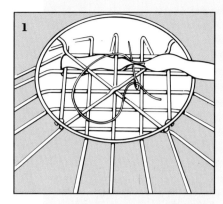

2 *Weave the base, then the first row of spokes around the base, ending at the first upright spoke worked. Wrap the ribbon around this spoke and continue weaving in the opposite direction. (It is helpful to secure the roll of ribbon with an elastic band to prevent it unravelling while you work.)*

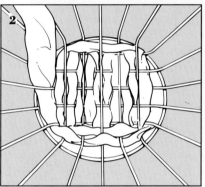

3 *Allowing the ribbon to scrunch up and always turning at the same spoke, weave the first band of colour, finishing at the turning spoke. Cut the ribbon 8 cm (3 in) longer than needed. Weave the excess ribbon back through the spokes and secure as before.*

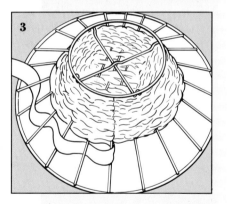

4 *Attach an approximate length of 13 m (14¼ yd) of 36 mm (1⅖ in) wide double satin ribbon in a new colour to the turning spoke. Secure as before. Continue weaving to the rim of the bowl, finishing at the turning spoke. Fasten off the ribbon as before.*

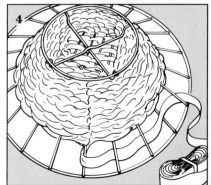

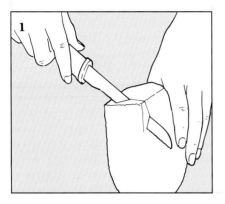

1 *Using a long bladed knife, shape a 10 x 10 x 15 cm (4 x 4 x 6 in) oasis into a pineapple shape. From 11.08 m (12¼ yd) of 25 mm (1 in) wide wire-edged space-dyed taffeta ribbon pin 11 m (12¼ yd) in a spiral from the centre of the oasis top down to the base centre using the method on p. 15.*

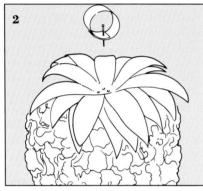

2 *Using the leaf template on p. 99, cut five pineapple leaves from stiff green paper. Curl each leaf section (see p. 14). Pin each leaf to the top of the oasis. Make a ring from an 8 cm (3½ in) length of the wire-edged ribbon and pin to the centre of the leaves. Scrunch the ribbon ring.*

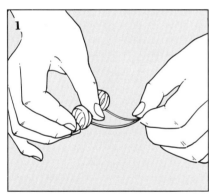

1 *For the grapes, attach 57 15mm (³⁄₅ in) diameter cotton moulds each end of 6.25 m (7 yd) of green wire cut into three lengths of 13 cm (5½ in), four lengths of 15 cm (6 in), five lengths of 17 cm (6¾ in), six lengths of 19 cm (7½ in), ten lengths of 21 cm (8¼ in) and five lengths of 18 cm (7 in). Cover the moulds using 30 cm (12 in) of 7 mm (¼ in) wide purple single satin ribbon (see p. 15) for each mould. Fold wire in half and twist.*

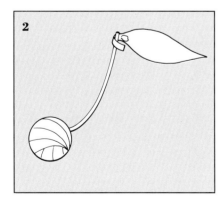

2 *To make a single cherry attach one cotton mould to 10 cm (4 in) of green garden training wire and cover with cherry red single satin ribbon as before. Gently curve the cherry stem. Using the cherry leaf template on p. 99, cut a leaf from 6 x 15 cm (2½ x 6 in) of stiff green paper and curl the leaf between scissor blade and thumb (see p. 14). Apply glue to the leaf stem and fold over the top of the cherry stem.*

1 *For the orange, cover a 70 mm (2³⁄4 in) diameter oasis ball with 6 m (6¹⁄2 yd) of 13 mm (¹⁄2 in) wide orange single satin ribbon (see p. 15). Cut out a fruit 'star' stalk from stiff green card using the template on p. 99. For an apricot or peach, use 4 m (4 yd 13 in) of 10 mm (²⁄5 in) wide single satin ribbon in apricot or peach to cover a 50 mm (2 in) diameter cotton mould. Pin a 'star' stalk to the peach only.*

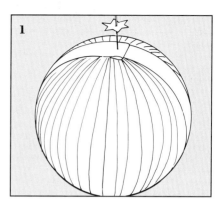

1 *For the cherries, attach a 15 mm (³⁄5 in) diameter cotton mould onto each end of a 20 cm (8 in) length of green garden wire. Using 30 cm (12 in) of 7 mm (¹⁄4 in) wide cherry red single satin ribbon for each cherry, spread PVA medium over the wrong side of each length and use to cover the moulds (see p. 15). Fold the wire in half then cross the ends over at the fold to form a loop. Bend the cherry stems to curve in the same direction.*

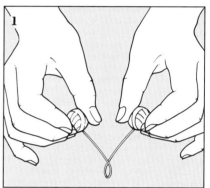

2 *Attach a 15 mm (³⁄5 in) diameter cotton mould to one end of 27 cm (10 in) of garden wire for the main stalk and cover with 30 cm (12 in) of 7 mm (¹⁄4 in) wide purple single satin ribbon. Thread the main stalk twice through the stem loops of the three 13 cm (5¹⁄2 in) lengths of wire and, 4 cm (1¹⁄2 in) from the end bead, knot. Attach grapes at 4 cm (1¹⁄2 in) intervals up the main stalk in the order in which they were cut. Twist the stems to form the bunch of grapes.*

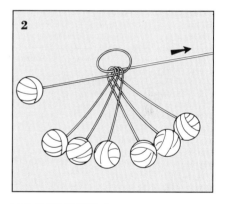

3 *Trim the main stalk to within 2 cm (³⁄4 in) of the top of the bunch. Using the template on p. 99, cut out two grape leaves from stiff green paper. Glue to the top of the main stalk and curl the tips of the leaves (see p. 14).*

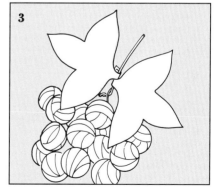

◀ *Let your imagination run wild with fruit that is always in season. This bowl of fruit will long outlast the real thing and looks far too good to eat!*

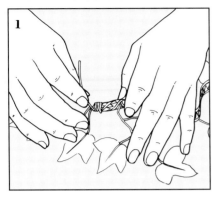

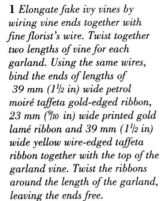

1 *Elongate fake ivy vines by wiring vine ends together with fine florist's wire. Twist together two lengths of vine for each garland. Using the same wires, bind the ends of lengths of 39 mm (1¹/₂ in) wide petrol moiré taffeta gold-edged ribbon, 23 mm (⁹/₁₀ in) wide printed gold lamé ribbon and 39 mm (1¹/₂ in) wide yellow wire-edged taffeta ribbon together with the top of the garland vine. Twist the ribbons around the length of the garland, leaving the ends free.*

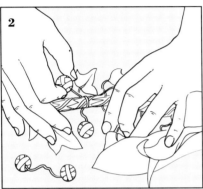

2 *Make pairs of berries using 3 m (3¹/₄ yd) of champagne, 6 m (6¹/₂ yd) of cinnamon and 7.2 m (8 yd) of ruby 7 mm (¹/₄ in) wide single satin ribbon for 54 berries (see p. 15). Twist the berries in small bunches around the ribbon and the vines.*

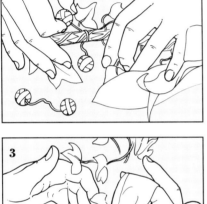

3 *Drape the garland and fix in place. Using all the wider ribbons together and cutting extra long lengths, tie large bows (see p. 23) at the focal points. Trim bow ends to different lengths.*

▶ *Fake ivy vines are perfect for an extravagant garland and carry none of the risks of poisonous ivy berries.*

1 Treat a 50 cm (20 in) length of 75 mm (3 in) wide gold double satin ribbon with PVA solution (see p. 13), squeezing off any excess and hanging up until completely dry. Use a craft knife or long-bladed bread knife to cut a 9 cm (3$\frac{1}{2}$ in) diameter circle from a piece of dry oasis 2.5 cm (1 in) thick. Shape the circle on one side into a dome curving down to sides 1 cm ($\frac{2}{5}$ in) thick.

2 Pin a 10 x 32 cm (4 x 13 in) strip of green crêpe paper around the side of the oasis, allowing 1 cm ($\frac{1}{2}$ in) of paper to show above the edge of the domed side of the oasis. Pin the extra 1 cm ($\frac{1}{2}$ in) flat against the surface.

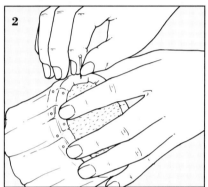

3 Use the sunflower petal template on p. 99 to cut a string of adjoining petals from the treated ribbon, snipping down between the petals almost to the ribbon edge. Pin the string of petals over the border of crêpe paper around the oasis dome. Using 100 cm (40 in) of 23 mm ($\frac{9}{10}$ in) wide spaced-dyed taffeta wire-edged ribbon, pin the ribbon to the central area of the dome in a spiral using the scrunch method on p. 15.

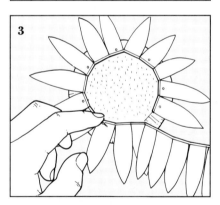

4 Bend 5 cm (2 in) at the end of three 45 cm (18 in) long florist stub wires to a slight angle then push the bent ends into the centre of the flat side of the oasis. Gather up the crêpe paper at the back of the dome and hold with one hand against the stub wires above where they bend. Bind the gathered edges of the paper to the stub wires with florist's tape, continuing binding down the length of the wires. Use the curling method on p. 14 to curl the petals.

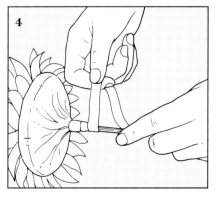

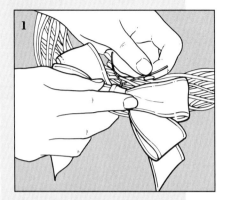

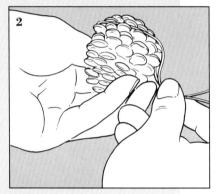

1 *Spray a 29 cm (11½ in) diameter vine ring and six fir cones with gold paint. Make six fake double bows (see p. 22) from 6.6 m (7 yd 12 in) of 39 mm (1½ in) wide green metallic-edge moiré taffeta ribbon, cutting two 35 cm (14 in) lengths for the loops, a 30 cm (12 in) length for each tail and a 10 cm (4 in) length for each knot. Thread florist's fine wire through each bow and attach to the vine ring by twisting the wire ends.*

2 *Wind 30 cm (12 in) of florist's wire around the base of each fir cone. Make six loose rosebuds (see p. 19) from 3 m (3¼ yd) of 39 mm (1½ in) wide purple taffeta ribbon without stems. Using 11 m (12 yd) of 7 mm (¼ in) wide cinammon single satin ribbon, make six bunches each of three pairs of berries (see p. 15). Attach the fir cones, roses and berries to the vine ring between bows by twisting the wire.*

3 *Cut 6 m (6 yd 24 in) of 3 mm (¹/₁₀ in) wide gold all-metallic grosgrain ribbon into 25 cm (10 in) lengths and knot through the bow loops to the vine ring, allowing the ends to trail. Tie small bows between the large bows using 3 m (3¹/₄ yd) of 9 mm (²/₅ in) wide gold all-metallic grosgrain ribbon cut into 50 cm (20 in) lengths. Cut the ribbon ends at angles.*

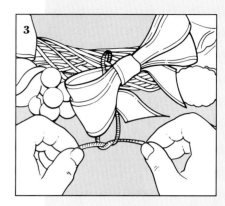

1 *Spray paint in green a 20 cm (8 in) vine ring and a disc of thick card cut slightly smaller than the vine ring. Lightly spray with gold paint in short bursts, holding the can about 30 cm (12 in) from the ring and disc. Attach the card disc to the vine ring using florist's fine wire.*

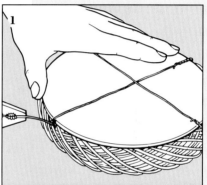

2 *Make a fake double bow and a fake single bow from 2.15 m (2¹/₂ yd) of 39 mm (1¹/₂ in) wide metallic-edge moiré ribbon cut into three 35 cm (13³/₄ in) lengths for the loops, two 45 cm (17³/₄ in) lengths for the ties and two 10 cm (4 in) lengths for the knots. Use florist's fine wire to twist onto the vine ring. Using 3.6 m (4 yd) of brown and 3 m (3 yd 12 in) of wine-coloured 7 mm (¹/₄ in) wide single satin ribbon, make 11 pairs of berries (see p. 15), divide into three bunches and attach to the vine ring. Cut 2 m (2 yd 4 in) of 3 mm (¹/₁₀ in) wide gold all-metallic grosgrain ribbon into six lengths and knot through the bow loops and vine ring, trail ends and cut at angles.*

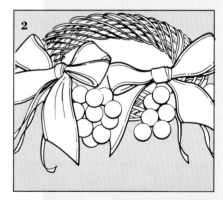

3 *Arrange the candles inside the vine ring onto the card base. Fix in place with a couple of wax spots on the sides and base of each candle.*

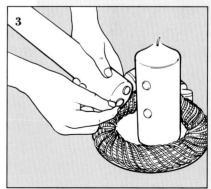

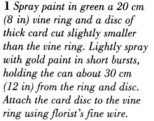

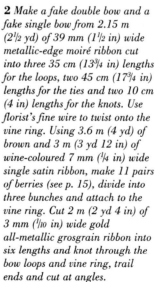

Accessories

Adorn old favourite hats and shoes with unusual ribbons or make a
stylish evening bag to create a new feel for your outfits.
Make sure your bridesmaids have the ultimate in trimmings
by sewing satin ribbon to their shoes and creating
the prettiest bridal pomander.

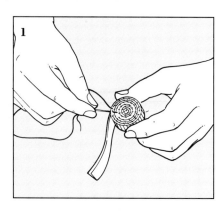

1 *Press under a turning of 1 cm (²/₅ in) at each end of a 70 cm (27¹/₂ in) length of 23 mm (⁹/₁₀ in) wide lilac petersham ribbon. Fold the ribbon in half lengthways with the turned ends to the inside and press. Tightly roll up the folded strip and stitch the ribbon edges together.*

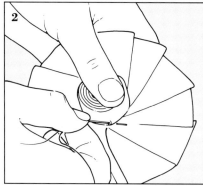

2 *From a 2.1 m (2yd 11 in) length of 50 mm (2 in) wide lilac petersham ribbon cut a length of 60 cm (24 in) to make a basic pleated rosette (see p. 21). Using tiny stitches, sew the petersham coil with the folded edge uppermost to the the centre of the rosette. Try on a basic straw hat with a crown approximately 55 cm (22 in) in diameter and mark the position for the rosette on the side.*

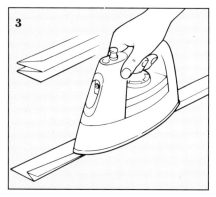

3 *Press the remaining 150 cm (59 in) of 50 mm (2 in) wide lilac petersham ribbon in half lengthways, then press the edges back to the centre fold so the ribbon is pleated lengthways in four and forms a zigzag effect. Cut the ribbon in half for two 75 cm (29¹/₂ in) pleated strips.*

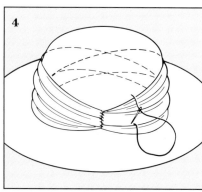

4 *Beginning at the rosette position, pin one pleated length of petersham around the hat, taking it up at the front by 6 cm (2¹/₄ in) and down to brim level at the back. Letting the pleats stand away from the crown slightly and using tiny stitches spaced along the indented pleated line, stitch the ribbon in place. Sew the second length of pleated petersham around the crown, taking it down to brim level at the front and up by 6 cm (2¹/₄ in) at the back. Neatly stitch rosette in place over the pleated ribbon ends.*

1 *Using 18 m (20 yd) of 56 mm (2¹/5 in) wide sheer ribbon in each of cream and green, fold over 4 cm (1¹/2 in) at the end of the cream and green ribbon laid on top of one another. Stitch to the centre of the flat crown of a wide-brimmed straw hat.*

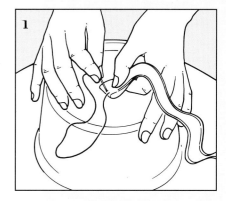

2 *Working round in a spiral and gently twisting the ribbons back and forth over themselves, sew the ribbon to the hat using tiny stitches spaced about 5 cm (2 in) apart. Take care to sew the ribbon close together so that the hat can only be seen through the ribbon and not between it. Covering any sharp edges that the crown may have, continue to stitch the twisted ribbon in a spiral around the crown sides and over the brim.*

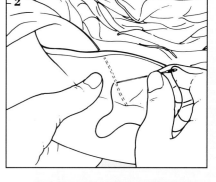

3 *Stitch the ribbon carefully over the brim edge so that the straw does not show between the ribbons. Finish by sewing the ribbon over the flap under the brim, taking care to stitch only through the flap and not through to the top of the brim. Stitch the ribbon to the edge of the brim if the hat does not have a flap.*

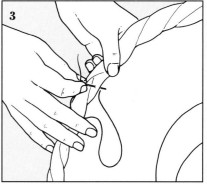

4 *From 3.2 m (3 yd 18 in) of 56 mm (2¹/5 in) wide violet sheer ribbon cut four 80 cm (31¹/2 in) lengths to make two tied bows in double thickness (see p. 23). Try on the hat to mark the bow positions at the side of the crown base. Stitch the bows in place using tiny stitches to hold the bow loops against the crown.*

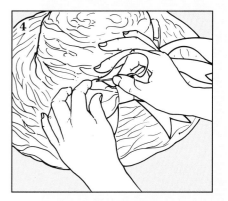

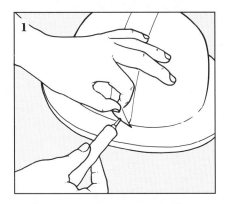

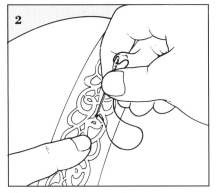

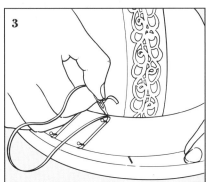

1 *From a 3 m (3¼ yd) length of 36 mm (1²/₅ in) wide wine velvet ribbon cut a length to fit over the crown of a traditional bowler hat from side to side. Stick down over the hat crown using fabric glue and leave to dry.*

2 *From a 112 cm (44 in) length of 30 mm (1¹/₅ in) wide gold braid cut a matching length to centre over the velvet ribbon. Stitch the braid in place, working through the braid, velvet and hat crown. Stick another length of velvet ribbon over the crown from back to front. Stitch a length of gold braid in place as before.*

3 *Beginning and ending at the back, wrap a length of velvet ribbon tightly around the base of the crown and stitch only the ends in place where they meet. Beginning and ending in the same place and taking care not to pucker the velvet, use a large-eyed blunt needle (a bodkin) to thread 2 m (2¼ yd) of gold Russia braid around the velvet band, starting at the back. Arrange the braid in diagonal lines about 3 cm (1¹/₅ in) apart and pin the braid in place as you work. Stitch the Russia braid to the crown each side of the velvet.*

4 *From the remaining velvet ribbon make a fake double bow without ties (see p. 22), cutting two 30 cm (12 in) lengths of velvet for the loops and 12 cm (4³/₄ in) of velvet for the knot. Wrap a 12 cm (4³/₄ in) length of gold braid around the bow knot and stitch the bow on to the back of the hat, covering the ends of the crown band.*

1 *Fold the brim at the front of a floppy felt hat up to the crown and fix in place with a few secure stitches.*

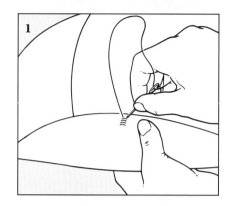

2 *Beginning and ending under the turned up brim at the front, swag and pleat 70 cm (27½ in) of 75 mm (3 in) wide bottle green double satin ribbon around the hat crown, pinning the ribbon as you go.*

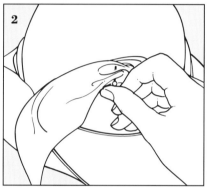

3 *Use small stitches to attach the ribbon to the crown, working through the ribbon pleats to hold them in place.*

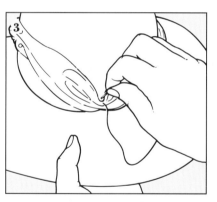

4 *From 7.2 m (8 yd) of 23 mm (⁹/₁₀ in) wide ribbon make 12 square roses (see p. 19). Use 6 m (6½ yd) of 36 mm (1²/₅ in) wide tartan taffeta ribbon to make six square roses. Arrange and pin the roses around the hat each side of the satin ribbon. Stitch the roses in place.*

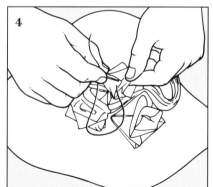

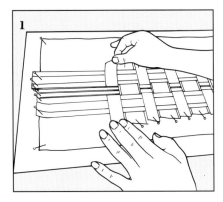

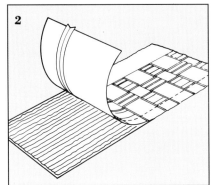

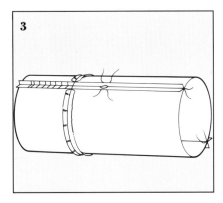

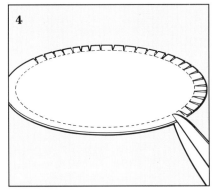

1 *Refer to the key on p. 97 for ribbon specifications. With right sides face down, pin two 46.5 cm (18½ in) lengths of the 9 mm (²/₅ in) wide ribbon onto a clean cutting board. Pin a 46.5 cm (18½ in) length of the 39 mm (1½ in) wide striped lurex ribbon either side. Weave 12 cm (4¾ in) lengths of the remaining ribbons through the grosgrain and striped ribbon following the weaving chart on p. 97.*

2 *Press 12 x 46.5 cm (4¾ x 18¼ in) iron-on interfacing onto the weaving and stitch 1 cm (³/₈ in) from the edges. From a 50 x 55 cm (20 x 22 in) piece of black velvet fabric cut two strips 4 x 24.25 cm (1½ x 9½ in). Take a standard 1 cm (³/₈ in) for all seams and press all seams open. With right sides facing, sew two short sides of the velvet strips together, then sew to one long edge of the weaving. Stick 14 x 46.5 cm (5½ x 18¼ in) of buckram to the wrong side of the weaving and velvet using PVA medium. Leave to dry.*

3 *Mark 9.5 cm (3¾ in) and 11.5 cm (4½ in) up from the lower edge on all four long sides of two 24.25 x 29.5 cm (9½ x 11¾ in) velvet rectangles. Matching marks and with right sides facing, stitch the pieces together along one long side, leaving a gap between the marks. Sew the lower edge of the velvet to the weaving. With right sides together, stitch the rectangle of velvet and weaving together, leaving a gap between the marks.*

4 *From a 24.5 x 66.5 cm (9½ x 26 in) square of black lining fabric cut a 16 cm (6¼ in) diameter disc. Cut two matching discs in buckram and velvet. Glue the buckram to the wrong side of the velvet and leave to dry. Stitch around the velvet covered base 1 cm (³/₈in) from the edge and snip into the seam allowance. Sew around the lining disc and snip in the same way.*

5 *Cut a 24.5 x 46.5 cm (9½ x 18¼ in) rectangle of lining fabric. With right sides together, sew the short ends together. Press seam open. With right sides facing, stitch one long edge of the lining tube to the lining disc and press seam open.*

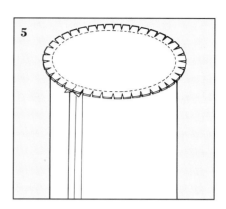

6 *With right sides facing, insert the lining into the inside-out velvet tube. Taking a 3 cm (1¼ in) seam, sew the lining tube to the unstiffened velvet edge. Trim the velvet seam allowance to 1 cm (⅜ in) and press the whole seam towards the lining. Turn the velvet and woven tube right side out over the lining, pinning 9.5 cm (4 in) of velvet still inside the tube in place. Turn the bag so the lining is on the outside and stitch along the seam through both layers, then work a second row of stitching 2 cm (¾ in) above through both velvet layers.*

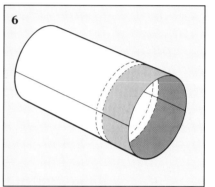

7 *Turn the bag right side out. Using a cloth, press the bag on the right side. Press the snipped seam allowance of the base to the wrong side along stitching, then press 1 cm (¼ in) of velvet along the lower edge of the bag to the wrong side. Stitching from the right side of the work and using double thread, oversew the velvet covered base to the bag.*

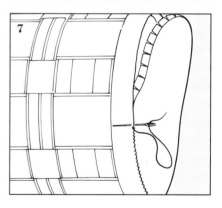

8 *Cut a 2 m (2¼ yd) length of furnishing cord in half. Attach a safety-pin to the end of one length and insert it into one of the gaps in the side seam. Thread it through the casing right around the bag and out of the same hole. Knot the cord leaving 12 cm (4¾ in) ends free, then knot each end separately close to the large knot. Fray the cord ends and steam press the threads. Thread the remaining length of cord through the casing from the opening in the opposite seam and knot as before. Oversew along the folded edges of the openings to hold them in place.*

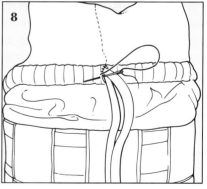

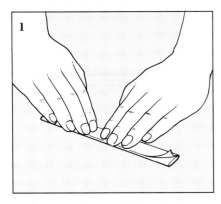

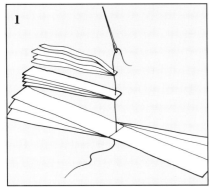

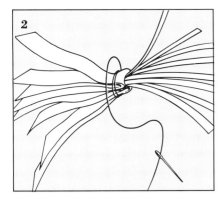

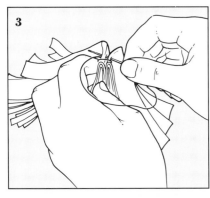

1 *From 110 cm (43¾ in) of 56 mm (2⅖ in) wide cream double satin or 39 mm (1½ in) wide blue gold-edged moiré taffeta ribbon make two fake single bows (see pp. 22-23) using for each one a 24 cm (9½ in) length for the loops, a 26 cm (10¼ in) length for the ties and 5 cm (2 in) folded in three lengthways for the knot. Fix a clip onto each shoe. Place the bow on the shoe, covering the clip. Mark the position of the clip on the back of the bow, remove the clip from the shoe and stitch to the bow. Neaten the ties with inverted snips.*

1 *From 2.64 m (2 yd 33 in) of 25 mm (1 in) wide black double satin ribbon for two pom-pom shoe clips cut three 22 cm (8¾ in) lengths and lay on top of each other. Fold in half widthways and bring the needle and thread up through the centre of the fold. From 4.8 m (5 yd 12 in) each of 7 mm (¼ in) and 1.5 mm (⅗ in) wide black double satin ribbon cut 24 lengths of 10 cm (4 in) in each width. Inserting the needle close to the ribbon ends and alternating groups of four lengths of 7 mm (¼ in)wide ribbon with four of 1.5 mm (⅗ in) wide ribbon, thread 24 lengths of each width onto the needle.*

2 *Fold three further 22 cm (8¾ in) lengths of the 25 mm (1 in) wide ribbon in half as before and pass the needle through the ribbons at the fold, so sandwiching the narrow ribbons between the widest ribbons. Wrap the thread around the base of the narrow ribbons, making the wider ribbons curl around them. Fasten off thread.*

3 *Attach a clip to a shoe. Fold the wider ribbons back onto themselves at the base of the bunch and stitch together along the folds. Stitch the shoe clip to the base of the ribbon bunch.*

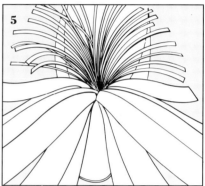

4 *Clip the ribbon bunch onto the shoe and fan out the 25 mm (1 in) wide ribbons over the shoe toe. Sew the ribbons in place near the base of the bunch, taking tiny stitches over the ribbon edges.*

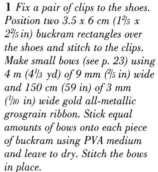

5 *Twist the 7 mm ($\frac{1}{4}$ in) and 1.5 mm ($\frac{3}{5}$ in) ribbons to form a spray. Make another shoe clip, attach the clips to the shoes and check both ribbon bunches are arranged equally. Trim all ribbon ends at angles, cutting the wider ribbons to avoid trailing them on the ground and cutting the spray of narrow ribbons to different lengths in order to make the dome-shaped pom-pom.*

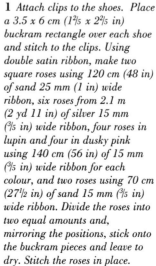

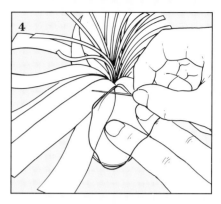

1 *Fix a pair of clips to the shoes. Position two 3.5 x 6 cm ($1\frac{2}{5}$ x $2\frac{2}{5}$ in) buckram rectangles over the shoes and stitch to the clips. Make small bows (see p. 23) using 4 m ($4\frac{1}{3}$ yd) of 9 mm ($\frac{2}{5}$ in) wide and 150 cm (59 in) of 3 mm ($\frac{1}{10}$ in) wide gold all-metallic grosgrain ribbon. Stick equal amounts of bows onto each piece of buckram using PVA medium and leave to dry. Stitch the bows in place.*

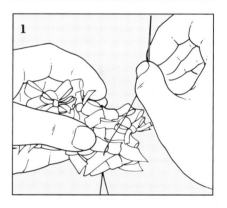

1 *Attach clips to the shoes. Place a 3.5 x 6 cm ($1\frac{2}{5}$ x $2\frac{2}{5}$ in) buckram rectangle over each shoe and stitch to the clips. Using double satin ribbon, make two square roses using 120 cm (48 in) of sand 25 mm (1 in) wide ribbon, six roses from 2.1 m (2 yd 11 in) of silver 15 mm ($\frac{3}{5}$ in) wide ribbon, four roses in lupin and four in dusky pink using 140 cm (56 in) of 15 mm ($\frac{3}{5}$ in) wide ribbon for each colour, and two roses using 70 cm ($27\frac{1}{2}$ in) of sand 15 mm ($\frac{3}{5}$ in) wide ribbon. Divide the roses into two equal amounts and, mirroring the positions, stick onto the buckram pieces and leave to dry. Stitch the roses in place.*

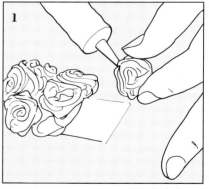

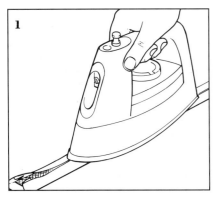

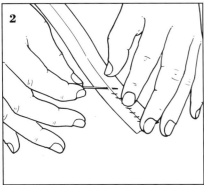

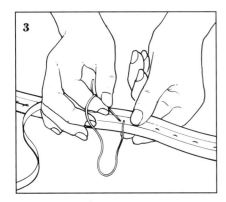

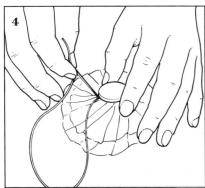

1 *To make the rosette headbands, centre a 5 x 45 cm (2 x 17¾ in) strip of iron-on interfacing over a 47 cm (18¾ in) length of 50 mm (2 in) wide double satin ribbon and press. Press a 1 cm (½ in) turning at each end of the ribbon over the interfacing. On the same side, press the long edges of the ribbon to the centre.*

2 *Slip stitch the ends of the ribbon closed. Slip stitch down the centre where the ribbon edges meet.*

3 *At each end of a 47 cm (18¾ in) length of 10 mm (⅖ in) wide double satin ribbon press and stitch 1 cm (⅖ in) double hems to one side. Stitch this ribbon right side up over the previous slip-stitched centre seam using groups of tiny stitches spaced 2 cm (1 in) apart.*

4 *From a 2.75 m (3 yd) length of 50 mm (2 in) wide and a 2.5 m (2¾ yd) length of 36 mm (1⅖ in) wide oyster double satin ribbon cut lengths of 50 cm (20 in) to make five basic pleated double rosettes (see p. 21). Cover five 29 mm (1⅛ in) diameter buttons with the remaining 50 mm (2 in) wide ribbon and stitch to the centre of each rosette (see p. 14). Sew a rosette each end of the band and, overlapping the rosette edges by about 1 cm (⅖ in), sew the remaining rosettes in between. Pin head-dress to hair using kirby grips. Make the same band using single gathered rosettes from 2.25 m (2½ yd) of 36 mm (1⅖ in) wide cream double satin ribbon, cutting lengths of 32 cm (12½ in) to make seven basic single gathered rosettes (see p. 20). From 4.2 m (4¾ yd) of 22 mm (⅘ in) wide peach double satin ribbon cut 60 cm (24 in) lengths to make seven square roses (see p. 19). Stitch in the centre of the single rosettes. Attach rosettes as before.*

1 *To make the pleated headband, take a 1.35 m (1½ yd) length of 50 mm (2 in) wide peach double satin ribbon and fold a 6 cm (2⅖ in) inverted box pleat in the centre of the ribbon. Pin 3 cm (1⅕ in) knife-edged pleats out to both ends of the ribbon. Turn under and press 2 cm (⅘ in) to form a double hem at each end. Steam press the pleats. Removing the pins as you work, tack the pleats and hems in place along the centre of the pleated strip.*

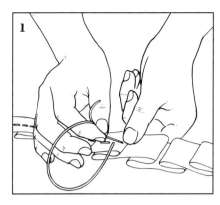

2 *At each end of a 47 cm (18¾ in) length of 10 mm (⅖ in) wide peach double satin ribbon turn over 1 cm (½ in) to form a double hem. With wrong sides together, sew the ribbon along the centre of the underside of the pleated work, using tiny stitches at each end and then at 2 cm (⅘ in) intervals along the length to hold the pleats in place.*

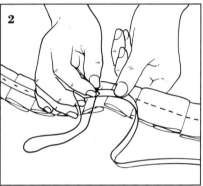

3 *Press 1 cm (½ in) hems to one side at each end of a 47 cm (18¾ in) length of 50 mm (2 in) wide peach double satin ribbon. Press the long edges of the ribbon to the centre. Using strip iron-on adhesive, steam press this folded ribbon strip to the top of the pleated strip along the centre.*

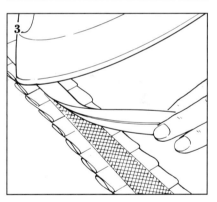

4 *Use 2.45 m (2¾ yd) of 22 mm (⅘ in) wide deep peach double satin ribbon to make seven square roses (see p. 19). Stitch one at the centre of the top strip, over the inverted boxed pleat. Spacing the remaining roses 6 cm (2⅖ in) apart, attach them to the centre of the band, stitching through all layers. Pin head-dress to hair using kirby grips.*

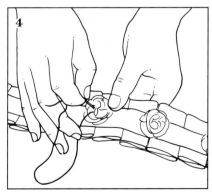

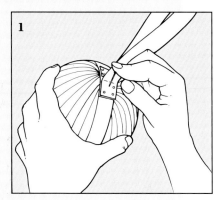

1 Cover a grapefruit-sized oasis with 5 m (5½ yd) of 23 mm (⁹/₁₀ in) wide pale peach single satin ribbon, securing the ends with pins (see p.15). From 12.22 m (13 yd 14 in) of 23 mm (⁹/₁₀ in) wide deep peach double satin ribbon cut 50 cm (20 in) for a hanging loop. Fold back 2 cm (¾ in) at each end. Placing the folds back to back at the top of the oasis, secure with pins.

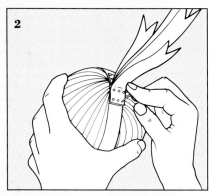

2 Folding and pinning the ribbons as for the hanging loop, attach two 30 cm (12 in) lengths of the same ribbon to the bottom of the oasis, directly below the hanging loop. Pin an 18 cm (7 in) length of this ribbon each side of the two longer lengths. Cut the free ends to form inverted snips.

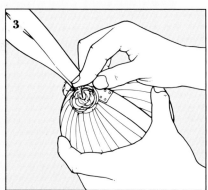

3 Use the remaining 10.76 m (11 yd 6 in) of the ribbon to make 17 square roses (see p. 19) and seven 8 cm (3¼ in) sashes neatened with inverted snips. Inserting a pin through the centre of each rose, pin a ring of five roses around the hanging loop and another ring of five around the 'tails' at the bottom.

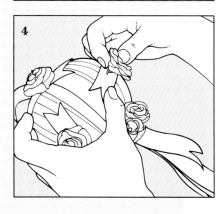

4 Push a pin through the centre of each rose and through the centre of a sash and pin in place around the pomander. Placing the pins under the folds of the petals, fix down the outer petals to the curved surface.

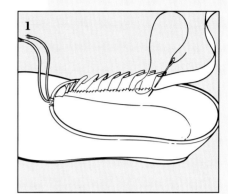

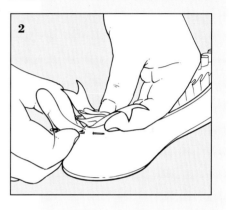

1 *Measure the circumference of the foot opening around one satin ballet shoe and multiply three and a half times for the required amount of 15 mm (3½ in) wide deep peach double satin ribbon for each shoe. Fold 1 cm (²/₅ in) to form a double hem one end of the ribbon.*

Beginning at the strings at the shoe front and forming 1 cm (²/₅ in) knife-edge pleats, stitch the ribbon around the inside edge of the string casing. Trim the ribbon to 1 cm (²/₅ in) longer than needed and neaten, folding 1 cm (²/₅ in) over to a double hem.

2 *From 136 cm (53½ in) of 23 mm (⁹/₁₀ in) wide deep peach double satin ribbon make two square roses for the shoes (see p. 19) using 60 cm (24 in) of ribbon for each. Using the same ribbon, make two 8 cm (3¼ in) sashes with inverted snips and stitch a rose to the centre of each sash. Sew a rose and sash to each shoe, covering the hems of the pleating and the shoe strings.*

◄ *Let your bridesmaids step out in the prettiest shoes by trimming them with pleated ribbon and a rose and sash to match your chosen colour scheme. Add a pomander as a glorious alternative to the usual fresh flowers and they will have a permanent reminder of their big day.*

Clever Clothing

Dress up the classic garments in your wardrobe with ribbon trimmings or make completed new garments entirely from ribbon. Add flair and fun with brightly-coloured ribbon, sophistication with gold braid and plaited ribbon, and do not neglect the occasional dash of wit with dotted ribbons and surprise motifs on the back of your garments.

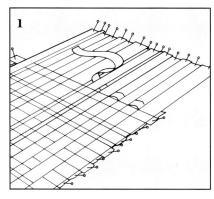

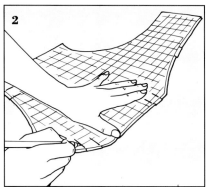

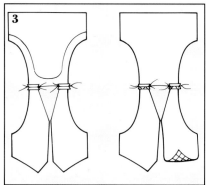

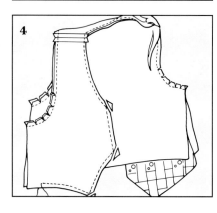

1 *Draw a 40 x 70 cm (15³/4 x 25³/5 in) rectangle on paper and pin to a cutting board. Refer to the key on p. 98 for ribbon specifications. Repeating the weaving plan on p. 98 four times up the length, pin the warp ribbons in place right sides down. Weave the weft ribbons. Reversing the weaving order for the warp ribbons, weave another rectangle. Press lightweight iron-on interfacing onto the rectangles.*

2 *Enlarge the patterns on pp.102-103 onto dressmaker's pattern paper. Pin the left front pattern to the right side of one rectangle, placing the front edge along the outer edge of the wide dot ribbon. Cut out and mark the position of the velvet ribbons around the edge. Reverse the pattern and cut out a second front, matching the velvet ribbon with the marks on the pattern. Stitch around the fronts 1 cm (²/5 in) from the edge.*

3 *From 120 x 140 cm (48 x 57 in) of navy lining fabric cut two backs, one left front and one right front. Use the shaded area from the back pattern to cut out a facing from lightweight iron-on interfacing. With right sides together, join woven fronts to one lining back at the shoulders with a 1 cm (²/5 in) seam. Fuse the facing onto the wrong side of the remaining lining back and join to the lining fronts at the shoulders as before. Press all seams open.*

4 *With right sides together and taking a 1 cm (²/5 in) seam, stitch the waistcoat lining to the waistcoat around the armholes, across the back neck, down the fronts and along the pointed lower edge of fronts to within 5 cm (2 in) of the sides. Snip into the seam allowance along the curved edges and trim the corners at the points. Turn the fronts right side out through the shoulders, keeping them between the two backs. Press the fronts.*

5 *With fronts right side out, but still sandwiched between the backs, match the armhole seams of the waistcoat with those of the lining. With right sides facing, join the side seams taking a 1 cm (²/5 in) seam. Press the seams open.*

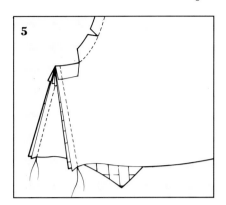

6 *Turn the waistcoat right side out. Press 1 cm (²/5 in) along the lower edge of the waistcoat back to the wrong side and then turn under 1 cm (²/5 in) along the lower edge of the lining. Slip stitch the lining to the waistcoat along this edge. Machine stitch along the lower edge of the back only, working 3 mm (¹/10 in) from the edge.*

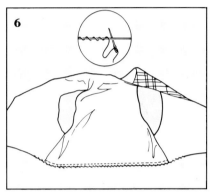

7 *Press 1 cm (²/5 in) around all four edges to the wrong side of two 9 x 32 cm (3¹/2 x 12¹/2 in) rectangles cut from lining fabric. Press in half lengthways with wrong sides together. Machine stitch around each tie, working close to the edges. Pin one end of each tie 11 cm (4¹/2 in) from the centre back and 11 cm (4¹/2 in) up from the hem, with the loose ties facing towards the centre. Stitch the tie ends to the back through all layers, stitching a rectangle 1 cm (²/5 in) wide with a cross within the rectangle.*

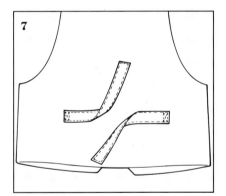

8 *Mark a horizontal buttonhole 1 cm (²/5 in) from the front edge and 5 mm (¹/5 in) below the beginning of the neck shaping. Mark the lower buttonhole 1 cm (²/5 in) above the beginning of the shaping for the lower edge. Mark two more buttonholes evenly spaced between the upper and lower ones. Stitch the buttonholes. Make corresponding positioning marks for the buttons on the opposite front edge and sew the buttons on. Use tiny dabs of fabric glue to hold the long loops of the jacquard ribbons in place where they cross each other.*

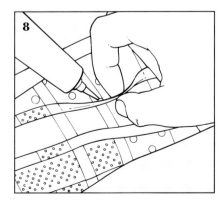

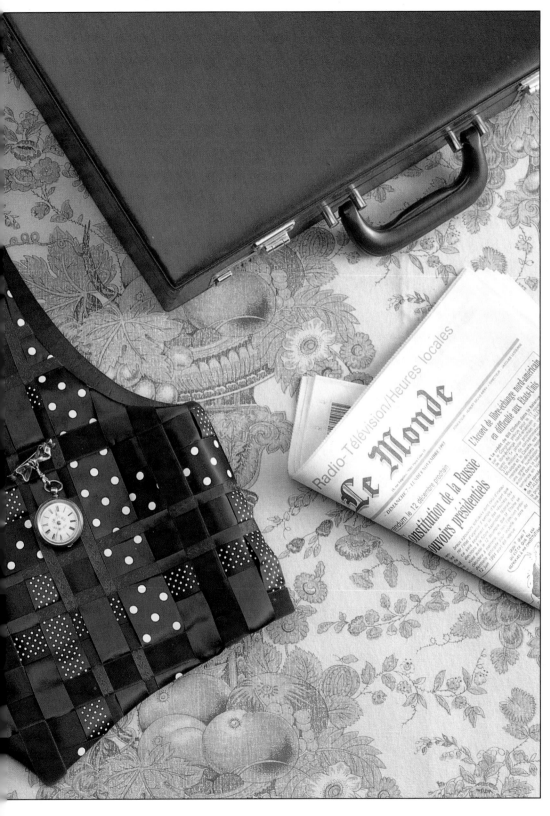

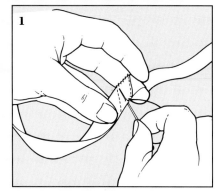

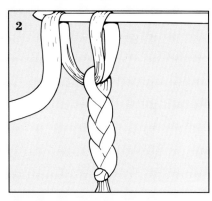

1 *You may need to join lengths of ribbon together for one long 40 m (43¼ yd) length of 15 mm (³⁄₅ in) wide double satin ribbon. Cut the ribbon ends at angles, overlap the ends by 2 cm (³⁄₄ in), then stitch together with slip stitch along the edges and a running stitch along the cut ends.*

2 *Tie a loop at one end of the ribbon and slip it onto an 8.00 mm crochet hook. Holding the hook in the right hand and the free long end of ribbon in your left, take the ribbon up behind, then over the hook. Draw the ribbon wrapped around the hook through the loop. Keeping the stitches even, continue taking the ribbon over the hook and pulling it through the previous stitch to form a long chain of crochet.*

3 *Lay a mediumweight sweater flat on a work surface and slip a thick piece of card between the garment layers to separate the back and front.*

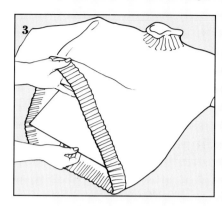

4 *Pin the crocheted chain in a spiral onto the lower right-hand side of the sweater front about 25 cm (10 in) from the side seam. Pin the chain in large petals around the spiral. Trail the ribbon out of the flower looping towards the right at waist level. Pin a spiral about 18 cm (7 in) below the right shoulder with petals around it. Take the ribbon over the right shoulder and pin a ring of large petals in the centre of the back, ending with a spiral in the centre. Carefully try on the garment to check the flower positions are correct.*

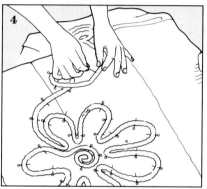

5 *Working through only one layer of knitted fabric, sew the crocheted ribbon chain to the sweater using a double strand of sewing thread. Stitch along the centre of the chain, working the stitches under the folds of the ribbon.*

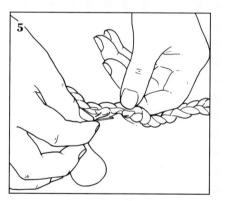

6 *Using a large-eyed blunt sewing needle, thread the ribbon ends at each end of the crochet chain to the inside of the knitted garment. Stitch the ends to the back of the knitted fabric with sewing thread.*

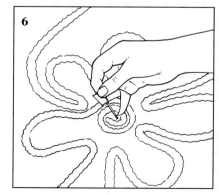

▲ *Why stop at the front? This large dramatic flower on the back will guarantee you a backward glance every time.*

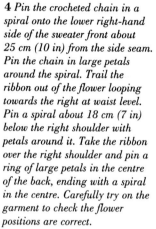

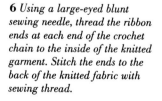

◄ *Trim any nautical sweater with crocheted ribbon that imitates twisted rope. Making a floral pattern with the ribbon rope is only one of many ideas: try a large anchor on the front, or even a skull and crossbones!*

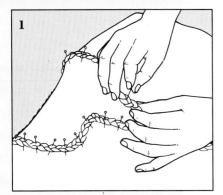

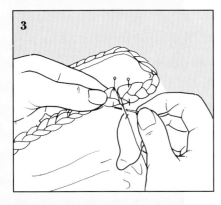

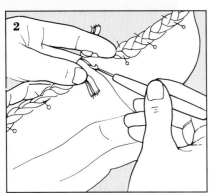

1 *Calculate the combined measurement of the jacket hem, both front edges, the neck edge, the cuff edges and the pocket flap top, adding an extra 30 cm (12 in) to the total. Using 65 cm (26 in) of ribbon for each 50 cm (20 in) required, plait lengths of 22 mm (⅘ in) wide double satin ribbon in cream, fuchsia and black. Leaving a 3 cm (1⅕ in) end of plait and beginning at one side seam, pin the plait around the hem and along the front and neck edges, taking care to ease the plait around any sharp corners. Trim the plait 3 cm (1⅕ in) longer than required and secure the ribbon ends by stitching at each end of the plait.*

2 *Using a seam ripper, carefully unpick about 4 cm (1½ in) of the side seam at the point where the ribbon ends meet. Tuck the plait ends into the open seam and pin. Stitch the plait to the jacket around the edges making tiny stitches worked into the folds of the plait.*

3 *Holding the seam edges together, slip stitch the opened side seam closed and stitch the folded edges of the plait together.*

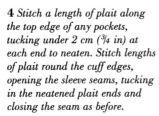

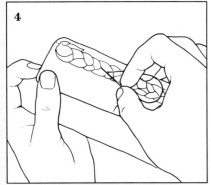

4 *Stitch a length of plait along the top edge of any pockets, tucking under 2 cm (¾ in) at each end to neaten. Stitch lengths of plait round the cuff edges, opening the sleeve seams, tucking in the neatened plait ends and closing the seam as before.*

▶ *All sorts of ribbons can be used to liven up the classic collarless jacket and make it suitable for both day and evening wear.*

1 *For the amount of Russia braid, calculate the combined measurement of the hem, front, neck and cuff edges and round all sides of any pocket, adding an extra 125 cm ($1\frac{1}{2}$ yd). Tucking the ends into a small opening in one side seam as before, sew gold Russia braid along the centre 5 mm ($\frac{1}{5}$ in) from all edges. Slip stitch the opened seam closed.*

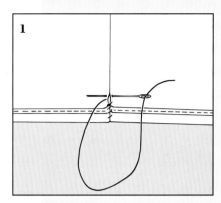

2 *From 75 cm ($29\frac{1}{2}$ in) of 50 mm (2 in) wide deep pink single satin ribbon cut a length 5 cm (2 in) times the required number of buttons. Steam press lightweight interfacing onto the wrong side of the ribbon squares. On the right side of the ribbon, draw a looped line about 1 cm ($\frac{2}{5}$ in) in diameter in the centre of the ribbon squares. Using the outlining method (see p. 14), back stitch 10 cm (4 in) of Russia braid along the drawn line. Cover the required size of buttons with the decorated ribbon squares (see p. 14) and sew onto the front edge of the jacket.*

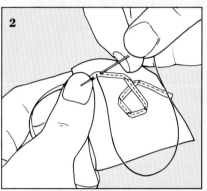

3 *Steam press lightweight iron-on interfacing to the wrong side of two appropriate lengths of deep pink ribbon, plus 1 cm ($\frac{2}{5}$ in) extra each, for the pockets. Press 5 mm ($\frac{1}{5}$ in) at each end to the wrong side. Draw a looped line along the ribbon working within 3 mm ($\frac{1}{10}$ in) of the short and within 1 cm ($\frac{2}{5}$ in) of the long sides. Using the outlining method (see p. 14), back stitch about 30 cm (12 in) of Russia braid over the drawn line. Press.*

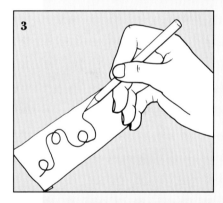

4 *Steam press the decorated ribbon with strip iron-on adhesive to the pocket flap. Beginning at the outer edge of the pocket flap and leaving about 5 cm (2 in) of braid extra, stitch Russia braid around the flap 3 mm ($\frac{1}{10}$ in) from the ribbon edges. Crossing over the ends, trim the braid 3 cm (1 in) longer than the edges of the pocket and stitch to the underneath of the pocket flap.*

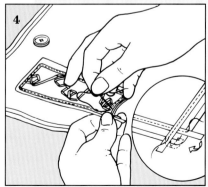

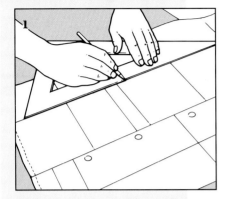

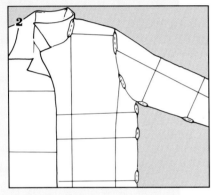

1 *Referring to the chart on pp. 104-105, use a vanishing marker pen to draw the ribbon positioning lines onto a cotton or cotton polyester long sleeved shirt measuring approximately 105 cm (41 in) round and 75 cm (29½ in) long.*

2 *At the side, collar, armhole and cuff seams on the back and front of the shirt unpick about 2.5 cm (1 in) of the seam above and 5 mm (⅕ in) below each horizontal line. At the shoulder, collar and sleeve seams unpick 2.5 cm (1 in) to the right and 5 mm (⅕ in) to the left of each vertical line.*

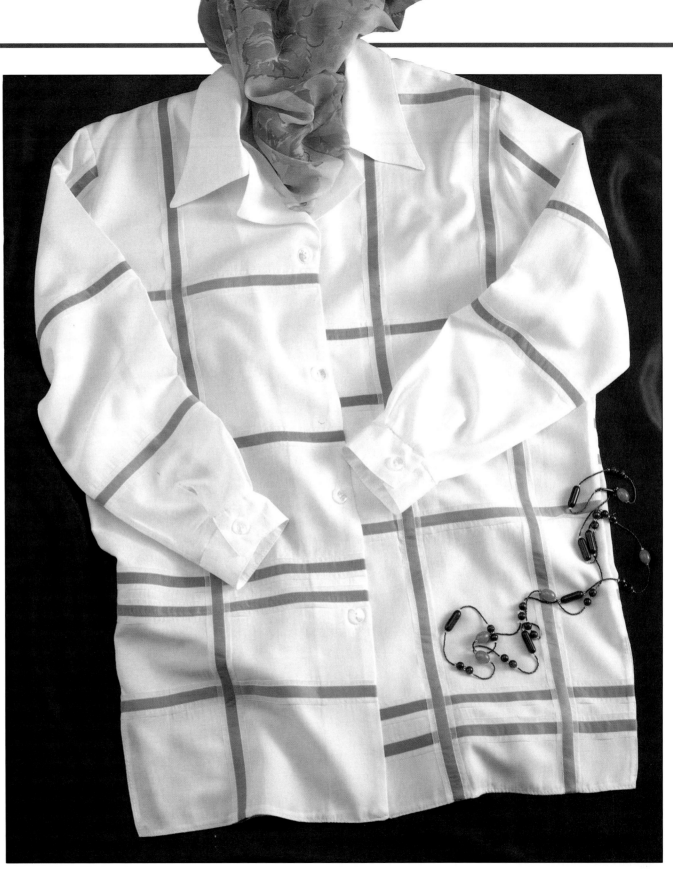

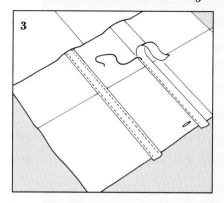

3 *From 16 m (17½ yd) of 22 mm (⅘ in) wide white sheer ribbon with woven lines 5 mm (⅕ in) from each edge cut lengths of ribbon 3 cm (1 in) longer each end than required. Positioning the ribbon lengths above the horizontal positioning lines, machine in place with a straight stitch, stitching 5 mm (⅕ in) in from the ribbon edges along the woven lines. Sew from the hem edges and into the open seams.*

4 *Refer to the ribbon positioning plan on pp. 104-105 for colour positioning. From 10 m (11 yd) of jade and 6.5 m (7 yd 4 in) of lupin 13 mm (½ in) wide single satin ribbon cut lengths the same as the ribbon casing and thread through the sheer casings using a small safety-pin attached to one end of the ribbon. Press with a dry iron. Stitch lengths of sheer ribbon 3 cm (1 in) longer than required at each end to the right of all vertical positioning lines, taking care to keep the ribbon straight when sewing over the horizontal casings. Cut matching lengths of the jade and lupin 13 mm (½ in) wide ribbon and thread through the vertical casings as before.*

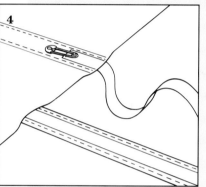

5 *Checking the ribbons are lying flat and are pushed into the seam openings, close the seams by machine stitching along the original seam lines on the inside of the shirt. Trim the ribbon ends to the seam edges. Neaten the seam edges.*

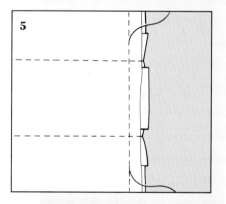

6 *Trim the ribbon ends to within 2.5 cm (1 in) of the hem edges. Fold the ribbon overlap in half then fold over the hem to the wrong side of the shirt. Slip stitch in place.*

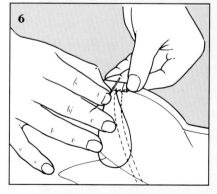

◀ *An individual touch can easily be added to the essential white shirt with coloured ribbons threaded through sheer ribbon casings. The softening effect of the sheer white ribbons means you will need to choose strong colours for the threading.*

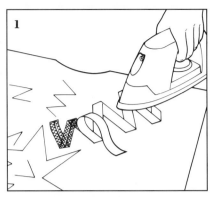

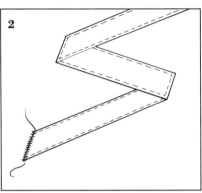

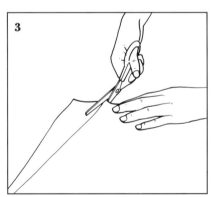

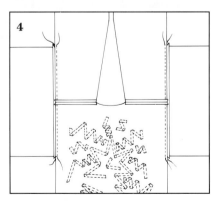

1 *From a 116 x 362 cm (45³/₄ in x 3 yd 34¹/₂ in) length of cotton poplin cut a 77 x 137 cm (30¹/₄ x 54 in) rectangle. Along one short edge mark two positions for the back neck 31.5 cm (12¹/₄ in) from each corner. Draw a curved line between these points, curving out to 2 cm (³/₄ in) from the edge. Cut along the curved line. Following the template on p. 104, draw the pattern onto the right side of the back, using a vanishing marking pen. Using 3.5 m (3 yd 31 in) of 22 mm (⁴/₅ in) wide double satin ribbon in orange and 5 m (5¹/₂ yd) in navy, press the ribbons to follow the zigzag lines. Fuse to the fabric using strip iron-on adhesive 2 cm (⁴/₅ in) wide. Cut the ribbon ends at an angle.*

2 *Using a straight machine stitch, sew the ribbons in place, working close to the edges and folds. Neaten the ribbon ends with a close machine zigzag stitch about 3 mm (¹/₁₀ in) wide.*

3 *Cut two 37 x 137 cm (14¹/₂ x 54 in) rectangles from the cotton poplin. Mark 5.5 cm (2 in) from the corner along one short end, then 55 cm (22 in) from the same corner along the long edge. Cut along the line between these two marks for the front neck shaping. Reverse the neck shaping when cutting the second front piece.*

4 *With right sides together, join the two front pieces to the back at the shoulders, taking a 1 cm (²/₅ in) seam. Press the seams open and neaten. Fold two 44 x 72 cm (17¹/₂ x 28¹/₂ in) rectangles for sleeves in half widthways. With right sides together and placing the folds to the shoulder seams, sew the sleeves to the back and fronts taking a 1 cm (²/₅ in) seam. Press seams towards the sleeves and neaten.*

5 *With right sides together, join the underarm and side seams taking a 1 cm (²/5 in) seam. Snip into the right angle of the seam at the underarms. Press the seams open and neaten. Turn up 6 cm (2¹/2 in) to the wrong side along the lower edge of the back and fronts and around the sleeves to form double hems. Machine stitch hems in place.*

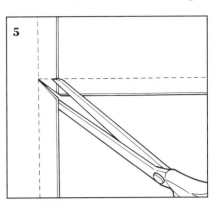

6 *Press two 12 x 150 cm (5 x 59 in) strips of cotton poplin in half lengthways with the wrong sides together. At one end of each folded strip mark a point along the fold 1 cm (²/5 in) from the edge. Mark a point 1 cm (²/5 in) in from the corner along the short edge. Draw and cut along the line between these points. Taking a 1 cm (²/5 in) seam and with right sides facing, join the shaped ends of the strips and press the seam open. Placing the seam to the centre back neck and taking a 1 cm (²/5 in) seam, stitch the border around the neck and down the front edges, leaving an extra 1 cm (²/5 in) of border below the front hem edge.*

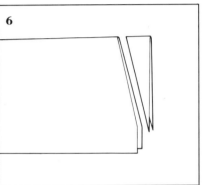

7 *Press 1 cm (²/5 in) to the wrong side along the remaining long edge of the border. With right sides facing, fold the border in half and stitch along the lower front edge with a 1 cm (²/5 in) seam. Turn the border right side out and machine stitch the long edge over the seam.*

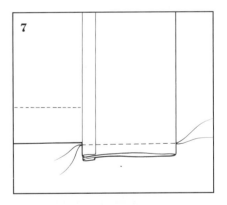

8 *Fold a 14 x 200 cm (5¹/2 x 79 in) fabric strip in half lengthways with right sides together. Sew a 1 cm (²/5 in) seam along the long edges and one short end. Snip the seam corners and turn right side out. Turn 1 cm (²/5 in) to the inside around the open end and press the belt along the seam. Machine stitch around the belt close to the edges.*

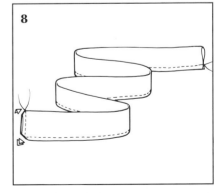

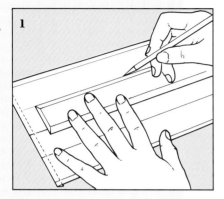

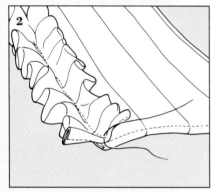

1 *Neaten both ends of a 112 cm (44 in) length of 12.5 cm (5 in) wide belt elastic with a zigzag machine stitch, then turn under 1 cm (²⁄5 in) to the wrong side and sew in place with a straight stitch. With tailor's chalk, draw a line 5 mm (¹⁄5 in) from each long edge on the right side of the elastic. Draw three further lines evenly spaced between the outer two.*

2 *Turn under and stitch 2 cm (³⁄4 in) to form a double hem at each end of 3.5 m (3¹⁄4 yd) lengths of 50 mm (2 in) wide double satin ribbon in yellow, orange, magenta, red and turquoise. Work a line of gathering stitches along the centre of each ribbon length. Pin the gathered turquoise ribbon to the right side of the elastic, placing the gathering stitches along one outer chalk line.*

◀ *Vibrant colours and carefree ruffles evoke the drama and passion of Spanish flamenco costume, creating a memorable outfit with gathered satin ribbons attached to a strapless evening dress. It can even be removed at a later date if required.*

3 Sew the ribbon to the elastic using a zigzag machine stitch and stitching over the gathering stitches. Gather the red, magenta, orange and yellow ribbon in the same way and stitch to the elastic next to the turquoise ribbon along the remaining lines in that order. Take care when stitching the ribbons not to stitch through the edge of the adjacent ribbons. Remove the gathering stitches.

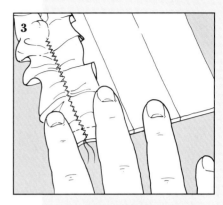

4 With right sides together, fold the elastic in half widthways to find the centre front and draw a line along the fold with tailor's chalk. Pin pleats in the elastic between the gathered ribbons measuring 6 cm (2¹/₂ in) either side of the centre front and 7 mm (¹/₄ in) in depth. Machine stitch the pleats securely, taking care not to stitch through the gathered ribbons.

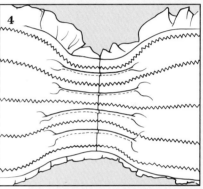

5 With the turquoise edge uppermost, pin the neatened elastic ends to the centre back edges and pin the centre front of the elastic down the centre front of the dress, leaving the band free at the sides for armholes. Pin the elastic to the top edge of the dress. Sew the elastic in place by stitching between the gathered ribbons and along the top and bottom elastic edges for 11 cm (4¹/₂ in), beginning 5 mm (¹/₂ in) from the back edges. Stitch elastic to the dress for 5 cm (2 in) from each end of the pleats and for 12 cm (4³/₄ in) from the centre front in each direction along the elastic top and bottom edges.

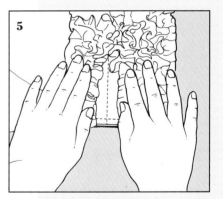

6 Make a peony from 150 cm (59 in) of 75 mm (3 in) wide black double satin ribbon, omitting the centre (see p. 20). Positioning the peony at the centre front of the dress on the gathered ribbon elastic band, sew in place, taking small stitches between the folds of the petals.

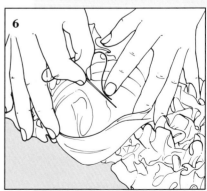

Gifts

Take advantage of the glamorous quality of ribbon to make sumptuous gifts for your friends. Personalize your presents by choosing colours and designs you know will delight, and present them in extravagant arrangements of the most dazzling ribbons.

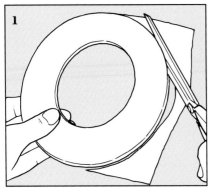

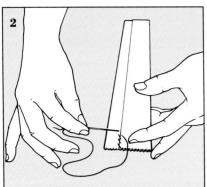

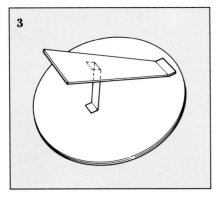

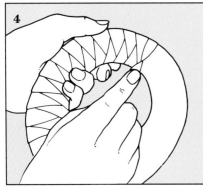

1 *Work on a protected work surface and use a sharp craft knife to cut the frames from mounting board. Use the template on p. 100 to cut two ovals, cutting out the centre from only one of them. Cut an oval picture stand (p. 100) and score along the dotted line. Using strong clear glue, stick the card ring onto 20 x 25 cm (8 x 10 in) of 1 cm (²⁄₅ in) deep wadding. Cut excess wadding from the inner and outer edges of the card.*

2 *Glue dark green fabric to one side of the other oval, cutting 1 cm (²⁄₅ in) extra all around and smoothing out any bubbles. Snip into the excess 1 cm (²⁄₅ in) and stick over the other side of the card. Cut green fabric 2 cm (³⁄₄ in) longer and twice as wide as the picture frame stand plus 3 cm (1¹⁄₅ in). Glue the stand onto the fabric and stick the excess fabric to the other side of the card. Leave the glue to dry then stitch the fabric edges in place.*

3 *Apply glue to the top of the frame stand above the scored line. Stick the stand to the fabric side of the covered oval, the corners of the wider end touching the edges. Leave under a heavy weight until dry. From 5.2 m (5 yd 22 in) of 20 mm (³⁄₄ in) wide tartan ribbon cut an 8 cm (3¹⁄₄ in) length. Apply glue to each end and stick one end to the underside of the stand 6 cm (2²⁄₅ in) up from the base. Stick the other end to the oval.*

4 *Glue one end of the remaining tartan ribbon to the card side of the padded frame. Wrap the ribbon round the frame, making one twist in the ribbon each time it passes over the wadding and overlapping the ribbon edges. Continue until the frame has been completely covered. Trim the end and glue to the card side of the frame.*

5 *Apply glue to a 1 cm (²⁄₅ in) border around the lower half of the card back. Stick to the frame front. Make a fake single bow (see pp. 22-23) with double ties from 103 cm (41 in) of 23 mm (⁹⁄₁₀ in) wide gold-edged wire-edged taffeta ribbon. Glue the bow to the frame.*

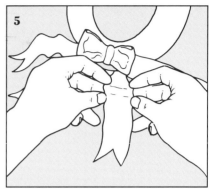

1 *Follow steps 1-3 to make a basic frame using the circular templates on pp. 100-101. Using 2.5 m (2¾ yd) of 23 mm (⁹⁄₁₀ in) wide black taffeta ribbon, cover the front as before but without twisting the ribbon. Glue a 5 mm (¹⁄₅ in) wide double hem both ends of a 1 m (39 in) length of 39 mm (1½ in) wide print lurex ribbon. Gather the ribbon along one edge with running stitches. Pin the stitched edge around the inner edge of the frame, starting at '5 o'clock'. Sew the ribbon edges to the frame and stick to the covered back as before. Fold a loop in the middle of 15 cm (6 in) lengths of both 9 mm (²⁄₅ in) wide and 3 mm (¹⁄₁₀ in) wide gold lurex ribbon. Stick onto the frame, covering the gathered lurex hems.*

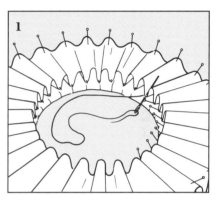

1 *Make a basic frame following steps 1-3 and using the square picture frame templates on pp. 100-101. Cut a square of green moiré taffeta fabric 2 cm (⁴⁄₅ in) larger than the front frame and apply glue to the wrong side of the excess. Stretch the fabric over the wadding on the front and stick the excess fabric to the back of the frame. Cut right into the corners of the fabric covering the aperture. Stick the triangular flaps to the back of the frame.*

2 *Stick the end of 4 m (4 yd 13 in) of 3 mm (¹⁄₁₀ in) wide gold and silver lurex ribbon to the back of the padded frame at one inside corner. Work three crosses along each side, wrapping the ribbon at right angles each end of the crosses. Glue the ribbon down at the back. Stick the lower half of the frame back to the front.*

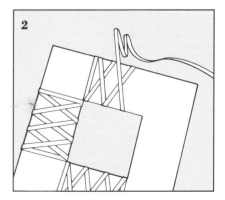

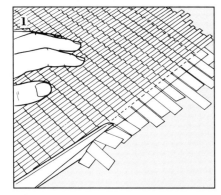

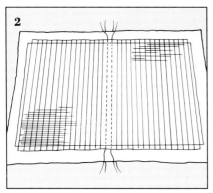

1 *Refer to the key on p. 98 for ribbon specifications. Draw a 31 x 48 cm (12²/₅ x 19 in) rectangle lengthways on paper and pin onto a cutting board. Pin 57 53 cm (21 in) lengths of green ribbon across the rectangle with wrong side up. Repeating the weaving plan on p. 98, weave 38 cm (15 in) lengths of the sable banana and sage green ribbon across these warp ribbons wrong sides up. Pin at each end. Press lightweight iron-on interfacing over the weaving. Stitch around the edges of the weaving on the right side. Trim the edges 1 cm (²/₅ in) from the stitches.*

2 *From a 38 x 75 cm (15 x 29¹/₂ in) piece of green moiré fabric cut a rectangle 38 x 55 cm (15 x 21³/₄ in). With wrong sides together, centre the weaving over it. Stitch along the edges of the central strip of banana ribbon to the edges of the weaving for the writing case spine.*

3 *Mitring the corners (see p. 13), turn under 1 cm (²⁄₅ in) for a double hem around a 5.5 x 7.5 cm (2¼ x 3 in) piece of moiré fabric for the stamp pocket and around a 14 x 33 cm (5½ x 13 in) piece for the envelope pocket. Sew the stamp pocket to the envelope pocket along the lower three edges. Press under 3 cm (1⅕ in) each short end of the envelope pocket. Press 1.5 cm (³⁄₅ in) of the fold back on itself. Centring the envelope pocket on the left-hand side of the case and working through the fabric layer only, sew the short edges in place. Stitch along the outer long edge of the pocket.*

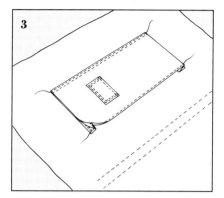

4 *From 2.07 m (2 yd 10½ in) of 25 mm (1 in) wide green petersham ribbon cut 26.5 cm (10½ in). Turn under a narrow hem each end. Stitch to the fabric 9.5 cm (3¾ in) from the upper and 2 cm (¾ in) from the outer edge. Lay the ribbon across the fabric to the spine stitching. Loop excess fabric and stitch along the right-hand spine stitching.*

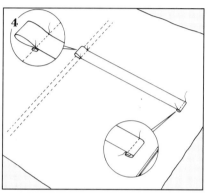

5 *Spray both sides of two 24.5 x 35 cm (9⅗ x 13¾ in) pieces of stiff card with spray adhesive. Pushing one long edge of each card up against the spine between the weaving and the fabric, stick the woven sides to the card. Stick the fabric to the other side of the card. Mitring the corners (see p. 13), turn and stick the fabric over the card edges.*

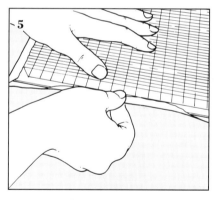

6 *Matching the edges of 180 cm (2 yd) of the 25 mm (1 in) wide petersham with the outer edges of the card, stick the petersham over the fabric and the weaving edges, neatly folding the corners at 45 degree angles to look like mitred corners.*

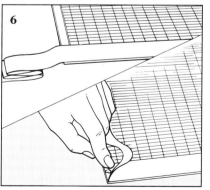

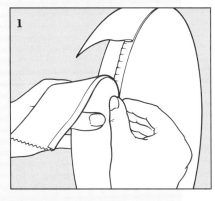

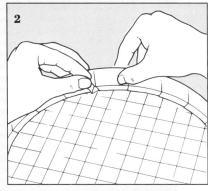

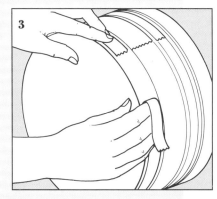

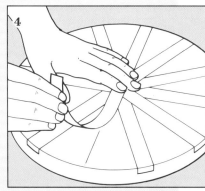

Measurements for ribbon amounts given are based on a hatbox with a circumference of 90 cm (35½ in), a depth of 14.5 cm (5¾ in) deep and with lid sides 3 cm (1⅕ in) deep.

1 *Use pinking shears to cut ribbon and fabric. From a 60 x 92 cm (23½ x 37 in) length of white moiré taffeta, cut and stick a 17 x 92 cm (6¾ x 36¼ in) rectangle around the hatbox sides. Fold the top edge inside and the lower edge underneath the hatbox. From a 45 x 92 cm (18 x 36¼ in) piece of thin white card cut and stick a 27.5 cm (10⅘ in) diameter circle onto the base and another to the inside. Line the inside with 14 x 92 cm (5½ x 36¼ in) of card. Cover the lid top with a 30 cm (12 in) diameter moiré taffeta circle, snipping and sticking excess fabric to the sides. Press 1 cm (⅖ in) to the wrong side along one long edge of an 8 x 92 cm (3⅕ x 36¼ in) strip of moiré taffeta. Stick to the lid rim with the fold along the top edge.*

2 *Fold and stick the lower edge of the strip to the inside of the lid, snipping where necessary. Line the lid with a 28 cm (11 in) diameter card circle.*

3 *With the lid on, use a vanishing marking pen to mark the ribbon width positions so they are evenly spaced between the lid rim and bottom of the base. Cut a 92 cm (36¼ in) length of pale pink 50 mm (2 in) wide single satin ribbon and cut a 184 cm (72½ in) length of 23 mm (⁹⁄₁₀ in) wide deep pink single satin in half. Use spray adhesive to stick the ribbon around the hatbox.*

4 *With the vanishing marking pen, draw a six-line star on the lid. Cut six 31 cm (12⅖ in) lengths from 3.7 m (4 yd 2 in) of 23 mm (⁹⁄₁₀ in) wide pale pink single satin ribbon. Stick the ribbon over the lines, sticking the ends flat against the sides.*

5 *Stick 184 cm (72½ in) of 23 mm (⁹/10 in) wide pale pink single satin ribbon twice around the lid rim.*

6 *Make seven square roses using 4.2 m (4½ yd) of 22 mm (⁴/5 in) wide deep pink double satin ribbon (see p. 19). Using strong clear glue, stick a ring of six roses around a central rose on the lid.*

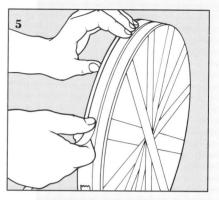

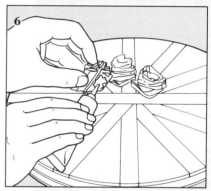

1 *Mark a line 3 cm (1⅕ in) up from the base around the hatbox. Stick 92 cm (36¼ in) of 75 mm (3 in) wide deep pink double satin ribbon around the hatbox above this line. Mark points opposite each other about 13 cm (5¹/10 in) apart along both ribbon edges. Cut 2.86 m (3 yd 6½ in) of 13 mm (½in) wide pale pink single satin ribbon into 11 cm (4½ in) lengths. Centring ribbon ends over the marks, stick lengths diagonally in one direction across the wide ribbon and then in the opposite direction. Cut the ends level with the wide ribbon edges. Cut two 92 cm (36¼ in) lengths of 10 mm (⅖ in) wide deep pink single satin ribbon. Stick over the latticed ribbon ends along each edge of the wide ribbon.*

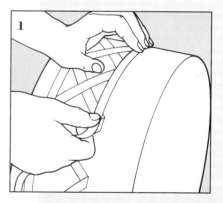

2 *Stick 184 cm (72½ in) of 23 mm (⁹/10 in) wide pale pink single satin ribbon twice around the lid rim. Using 2.88 m (3 yd 4½ in) of 36 mm (1⅖ in) wide dark pink double satin ribbon, make nine gathered rosettes (see p. 20) with 15 mm (⅗ in) covered buttons (see p. 14). Stick in a circle onto the lid. Make a double gathered rosette (see p. 20) using 50 cm (20 in) of 75 mm (3 in) wide deep pink double satin ribbon and 40 cm (15¾ in) of 50 mm (2 in) wide pale pink double satin ribbon with a 2.5 mm (1 in) button covered with pale pink ribbon. Stick in the centre of the lid.*

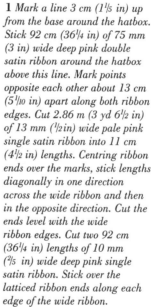

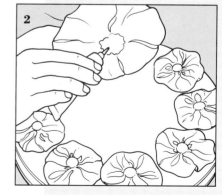

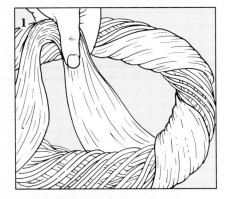

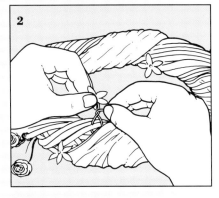

1 *Spiral about 130 cm (51 in) of pink paper ribbon around a 30 cm (12 in) diameter vine ring, leaving large gaps of vine showing. Trim ends and stick in place with quick-drying strong paper glue.*

2 *From 5 m (5½ yd) of 23 mm (⁹/₁₀ in) wide pink double satin ribbon make 14 rosebuds with stems (see p. 18). Referring to the instructions on pp. 16-17 and treating the ribbon beforehand in a PVA solution (see p. 13), make 18 anemonies using 100 cm (40 in) of lemon ribbon, seven bluebells using 60 cm (24 in) of blue ribbon and five sprigs of gypsophila using 30 cm (12 in) of cream ribbon - all in 50 mm (2 in) wide double satin ribbon. Thread each stem through the vine and secure. Make a fake single bow (see pp. 22-23) from 110 cm (44 in) of paper ribbon. Glue the bow onto the vine, covering the join of the paper ribbon.*

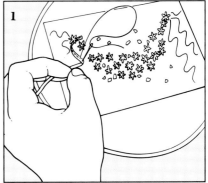

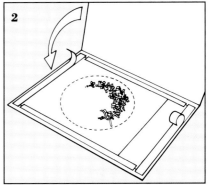

1 *Refer to the key on p. 107 for ribbon widths and lengths. Using dressmaker's carbon paper, transfer each embroidery motif on p. 107 onto the centre of 20 cm (8 in) square pieces of embroidery linen with 27 threads per 2.5 cm (1 in). Using an embroidery hoop and following the key on p. 107, embroider the motifs (see p. 12). Use tiny running stitches to stitch the ribbon in place on the garland motif.*

2 *Press the embroidery on the wrong side. Trim the embroidery linen to just smaller than the front of a blank card with a pre-cut aperture. With the right sides of the card and the embroidery face down, frame the embroidery within the opening of the card. Use double-sided adhesive tape along all four sides to stick the embroidery to the card. Use double-sided adhesive tape to stick the card backing over the back of the embroidery.*

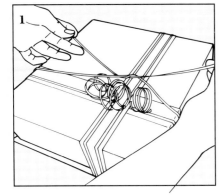

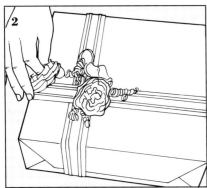

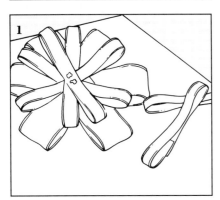

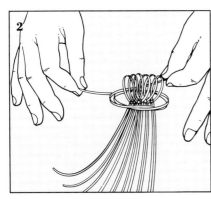

1 *Wrap 39 mm (1½ in) wide doubleface satin-edge grosgrain ribbon once around the parcel and fix ends in place at the back with sticky tape. Wrap ribbon around the parcel at right angles to the first length so dividing the top into one small square, one large square and two equal rectangles. Tie narrow foil gift ribbon around the package each side of the grosgrain section of ribbon, knotting it where the wider ribbons cross on top and leaving ends between 20 cm (8 in) and 30 cm (12 in) long.*

2 *Make three square roses using 3 m (3 yd) of 39 mm (1½ in) wide double satin ribbon (see p. 19). Use strong clear glue to stick the roses at the point where the ribbons meet. Leave glue to dry, then curl the narrow foil ribbon (see p. 14) and arrange so that the ribbon coils emerge between the roses.*

1 *From 111 cm (45 in) of 39 mm (1½ in) wide and 192 cm (78 in) of 15 mm (⅗ in) wide sheer lurex stripped ribbon cut three and six equal lengths respectively. Form loops by overlapping the ends by 2 cm (¾ in) and gluing. Flatten the loops with the join underneath and without creasing the folds. Stick the three wide loops on top of each other to form a star shape. Then stick the six thinner loops together to form another star. Centre and stick the thinner ribbon star on top of the wider ribbon star.*

2 *Securely knot a loop in the centre of ten 50 cm (20 in) lengths of 3 mm (1/10 in) wide sheer lurex striped ribbon, leaving 20 cm (8 in) ends to each length. Thread a 50 cm (20 in) length of the same ribbon through each loop and knot at the base of the loops. Wrap the ribbon back around the loops and securely knot at the back of the loops at the base. Cut all ribbon ends at angles to neaten.*

3 *Arrange the trailing ribbon ends to spray out from the base of the loops. Stitch the loop knots to the centre of the ribbon star. Wrap the 39 mm (1½ in) wide sheer lurex striped ribbon lengthways and then widthways around the parcel, gluing the ends together on top of the parcel. Glue the star to the parcel over the ribbon ends.*

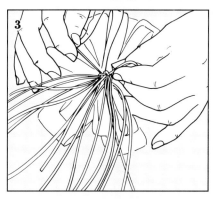

1 *Tie and knot a 60 cm (24 in) length of red narrow foil gift ribbon round an 11 cm (4½ in) deep crêpe paper bag. Alternating red and gold narrow foil gift ribbon, thread and knot 50 cm (20 in) lengths at 1 cm (⅖ in) intervals around the ribbon already secured. The trailing ends should be of equal length. Curl the ribbon ends (see p. 14).*

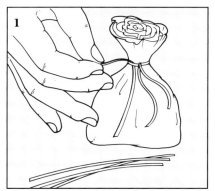

1 *Knot a 40 cm (16 in) length of 15 mm (⅗ in) ribbon around a 15 cm (6 in) deep crêpe paper bag. Fold 6 cm (2½ in) at one end of an 82 cm (33 in) length back on the main length. Continue folding the ribbon back and forth on itself at 10 cm (4 in) intervals in concertina style, ending with a 6 cm (2½ in) end. Stitch through the ribbon layers and ends. Tie the ribbon ends attached to the bag around the centre of the concertina. Stitch a square rose made from a 35 cm (14 in) length of the ribbon (see p. 19) over the knot.*

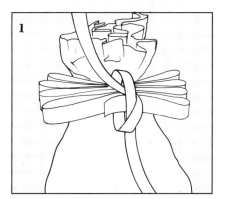

1 *Place the gift in the centre of a large, green crêpe paper square. Gather up the edges and knot together with narrow foil gift ribbon. Trim ends to 2 cm (¾ in). Using 50 cm (20 in) lengths of 23 mm (9/10 in) of wide print lurex ribbon for each bow and spacing them about 3 cm (1¼ in) apart, thread the ribbon behind the foil gift ribbon and tie in a neat bow (see p. 23). Trim bow ends and neaten with inverted snips. Using tiny strips of double-sided sticky tape, stick the backs of the bow loops together.*

TEMPLATES, CHARTS AND PATTERNS

The following pages present the templates, charts and patterns for the projects.

The ethnic cushion templates, the woven waistcoat pattern and charts A, B and C for the bedspread are printed reduced in size. Enlarge the ethnic cushion templates and the bedspread charts by 200% on a photocopier. Enlarge the waistcoat pattern by copying the lines square by square onto a grid of 2 cm (³/₄ in) squares. The flower, picture frame and gift card templates and the tablecloth motif and bedspread chart D are all printed actual size.

TABLE RUNNER
Page 48

All ribbons for the table runner are 22 mm (⁴/₅ in) wide single satin

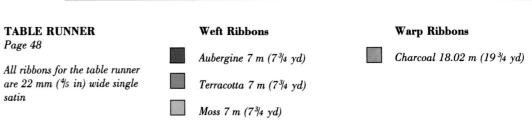

Weft Ribbons

Aubergine 7 m (7³/₄ yd)

Terracotta 7 m (7³/₄ yd)

Moss 7 m (7³/₄ yd)

Warp Ribbons

Charcoal 18.02 m (19³/₄ yd)

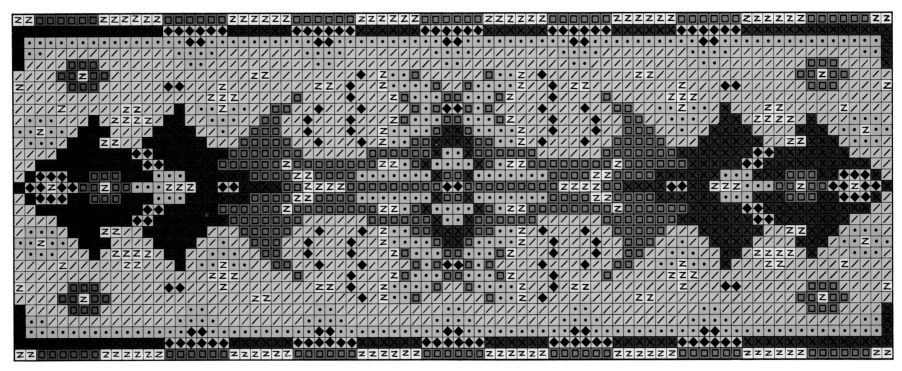

WALLHANGING
Pages 32-33

38 mm (1¹/₂ in) wide double satin ribbon

◆ Bronze lurex 9 m (10 yd)

36 mm (1²/₅ in) wide double satin ribbon

• Jade 20 m (22 yd)

╱ Airforce Blue 40 m (44 yd)

✗ Chocolate 18 m (20 yd)

▢ Terracotta 23 m (25¹/₄ yd)

Z Ochre 14 m (15¹/₂ yd)

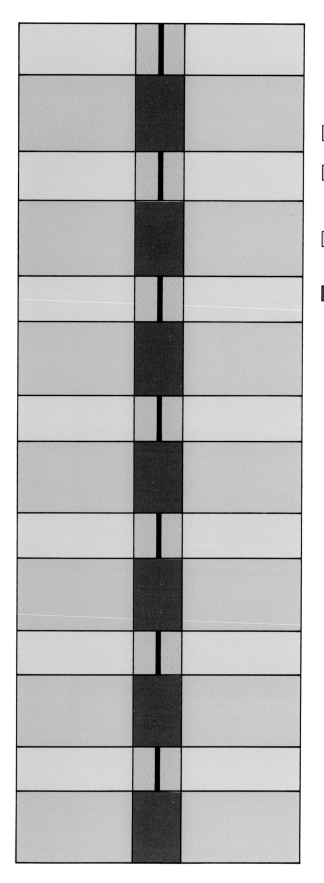

EVENING BAG
Pages 62-63

Warp Ribbons

39 mm (1½ in) wide black and gold stripe 93 cm (37 in)

9 mm (⅖ in) wide black-edged gold grosgrain 93 cm (37 in)

Weft Ribbons

23 mm (⁹⁄₁₀ in) wide black double face satin-edge grosgrain 84 cm (33 in)

39 mm (1½ in) wide black metallic-edge moiré taffeta

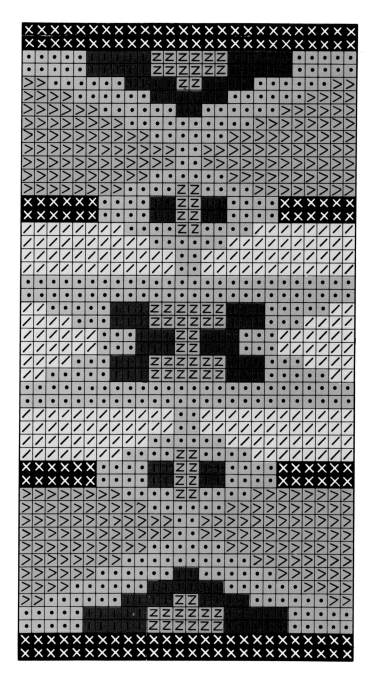

KEY CABINET
Pages 28-29

All ribbons for the key cabinet are 5 mm (⅕ in) wide double satin

☒ Black 4 m (4½ yd)

▷ Jade 2.5 m (2¾ yd)

⟋ Turquoise 3.5 m (4 yd)

• Fuschia 5 m (5½ yd)

■ Red 2 m (2¼ yd)

Z Orange 1.5 m (2 m)

WRITING CASE
Pages 88-89

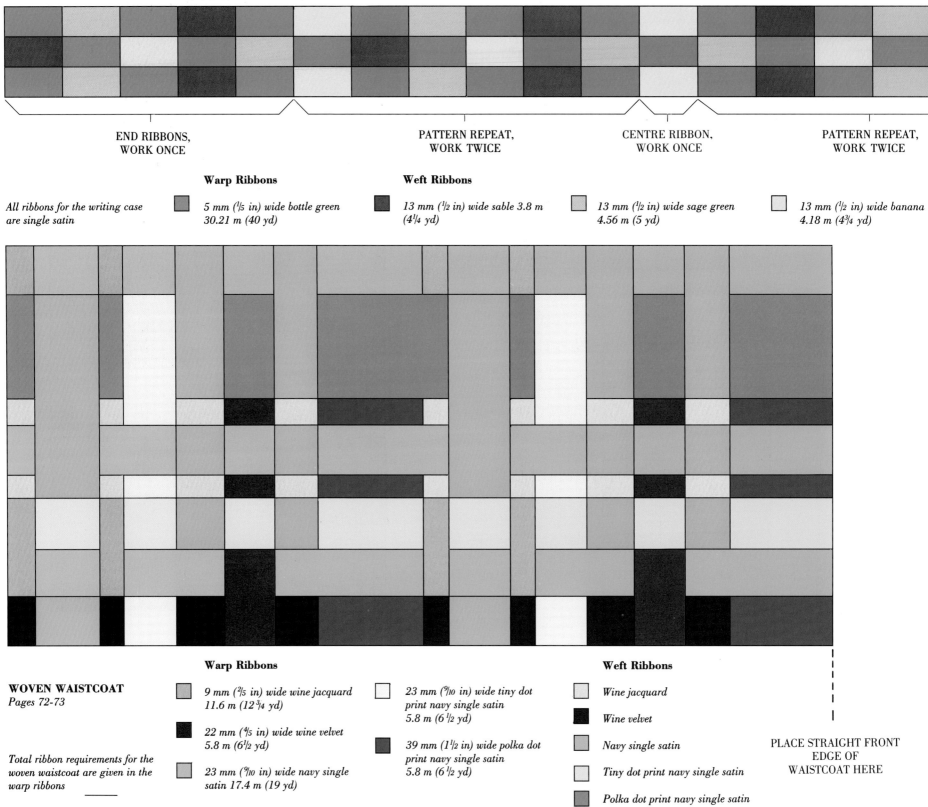

END RIBBONS,
WORK ONCE

PATTERN REPEAT,
WORK TWICE

CENTRE RIBBON,
WORK ONCE

PATTERN REPEAT,
WORK TWICE

Warp Ribbons

Weft Ribbons

All ribbons for the writing case are single satin

5 mm (¹/5 in) wide bottle green 30.21 m (40 yd)

13 mm (¹/2 in) wide sable 3.8 m (4¹/4 yd)

13 mm (¹/2 in) wide sage green 4.56 m (5 yd)

13 mm (¹/2 in) wide banana 4.18 m (4³/4 yd)

Warp Ribbons

Weft Ribbons

WOVEN WAISTCOAT
Pages 72-73

9 mm (²/5 in) wide wine jacquard 11.6 m (12³/4 yd)

23 mm (⁹/10 in) wide tiny dot print navy single satin 5.8 m (6¹/2 yd)

Wine jacquard

22 mm (⁴/5 in) wide wine velvet 5.8 m (6¹/2 yd)

39 mm (1¹/2 in) wide polka dot print navy single satin 5.8 m (6¹/2 yd)

Wine velvet

Total ribbon requirements for the woven waistcoat are given in the warp ribbons

23 mm (⁹/10 in) wide navy single satin 17.4 m (19 yd)

Navy single satin

Tiny dot print navy single satin

Polka dot print navy single satin

PLACE STRAIGHT FRONT
EDGE OF
WAISTCOAT HERE

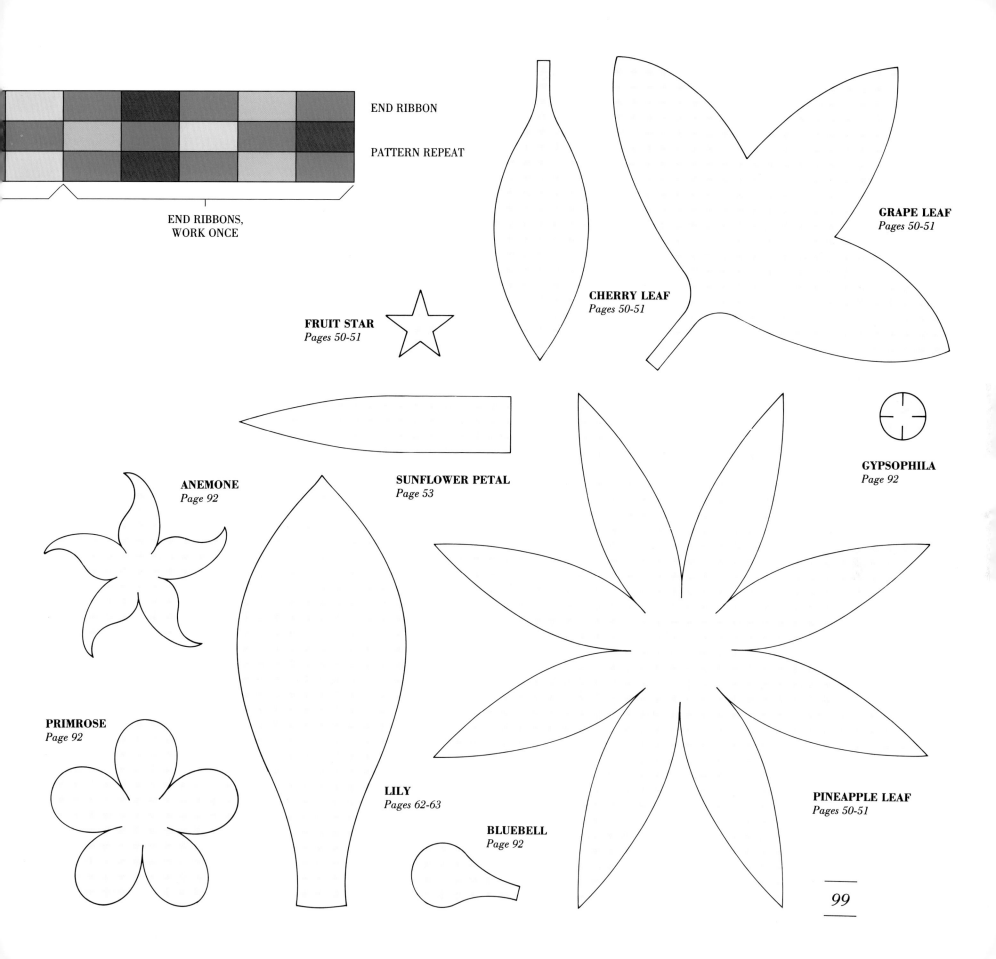

END RIBBON

PATTERN REPEAT

END RIBBONS,
WORK ONCE

GRAPE LEAF
Pages 50-51

CHERRY LEAF
Pages 50-51

FRUIT STAR
Pages 50-51

GYPSOPHILA
Page 92

ANEMONE
Page 92

SUNFLOWER PETAL
Page 53

PRIMROSE
Page 92

LILY
Pages 62-63

PINEAPPLE LEAF
Pages 50-51

BLUEBELL
Page 92

99

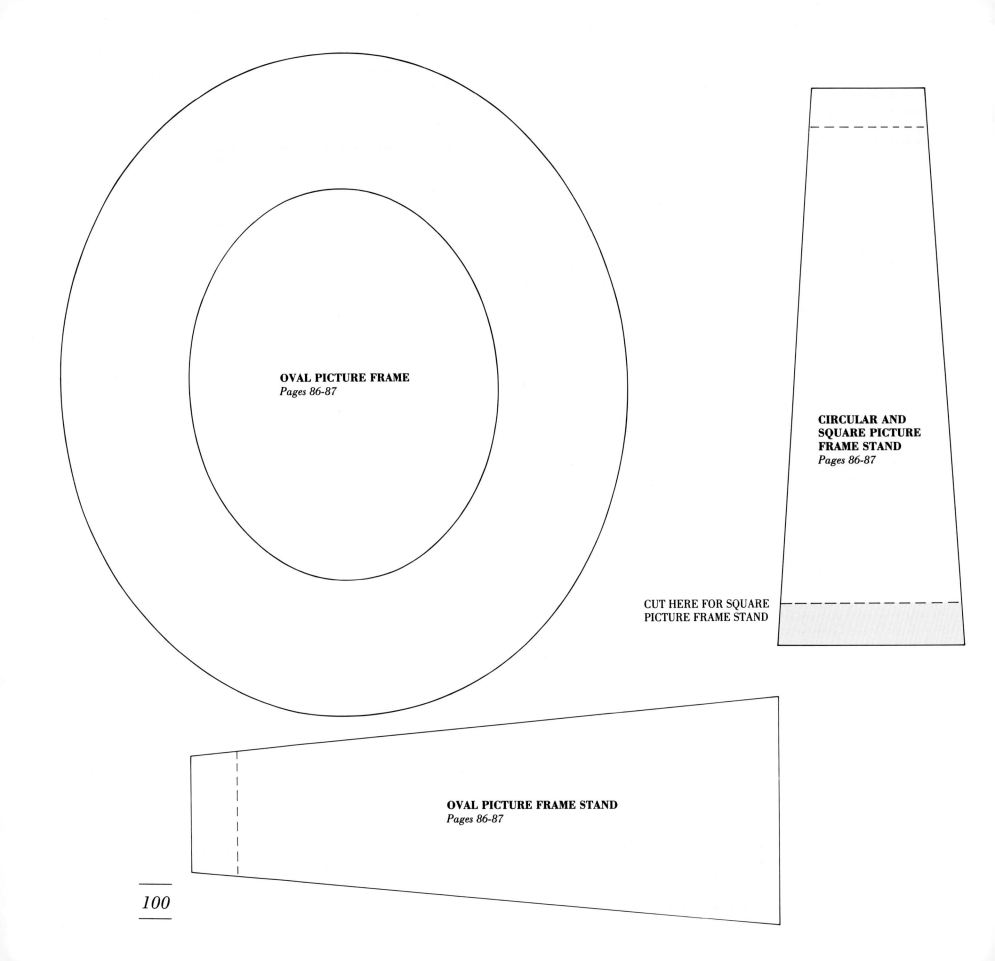

OVAL PICTURE FRAME
Pages 86-87

**CIRCULAR AND
SQUARE PICTURE
FRAME STAND**
Pages 86-87

CUT HERE FOR SQUARE
PICTURE FRAME STAND

OVAL PICTURE FRAME STAND
Pages 86-87

100

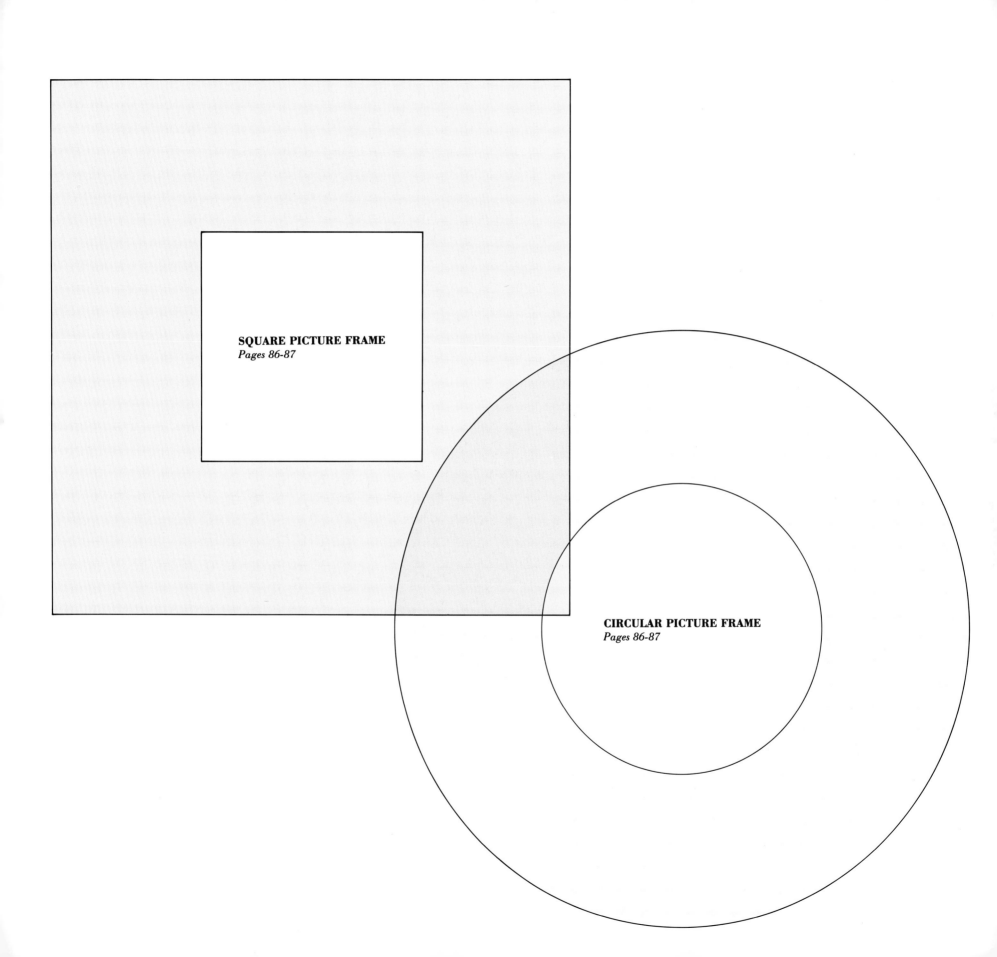

SQUARE PICTURE FRAME
Pages 86-87

CIRCULAR PICTURE FRAME
Pages 86-87

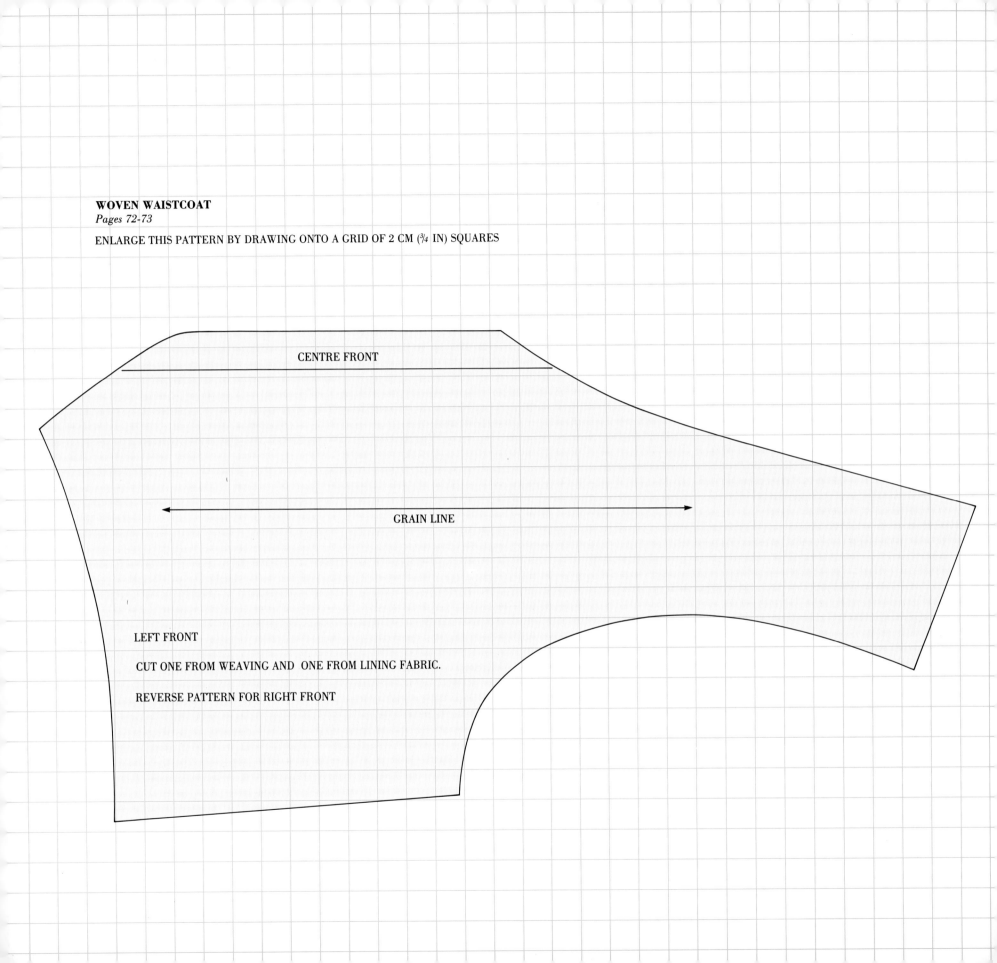

WOVEN WAISTCOAT
Pages 72-73

ENLARGE THIS PATTERN BY DRAWING ONTO A GRID OF 2 CM (¾ IN) SQUARES

CENTRE FRONT

GRAIN LINE

LEFT FRONT

CUT ONE FROM WEAVING AND ONE FROM LINING FABRIC.

REVERSE PATTERN FOR RIGHT FRONT

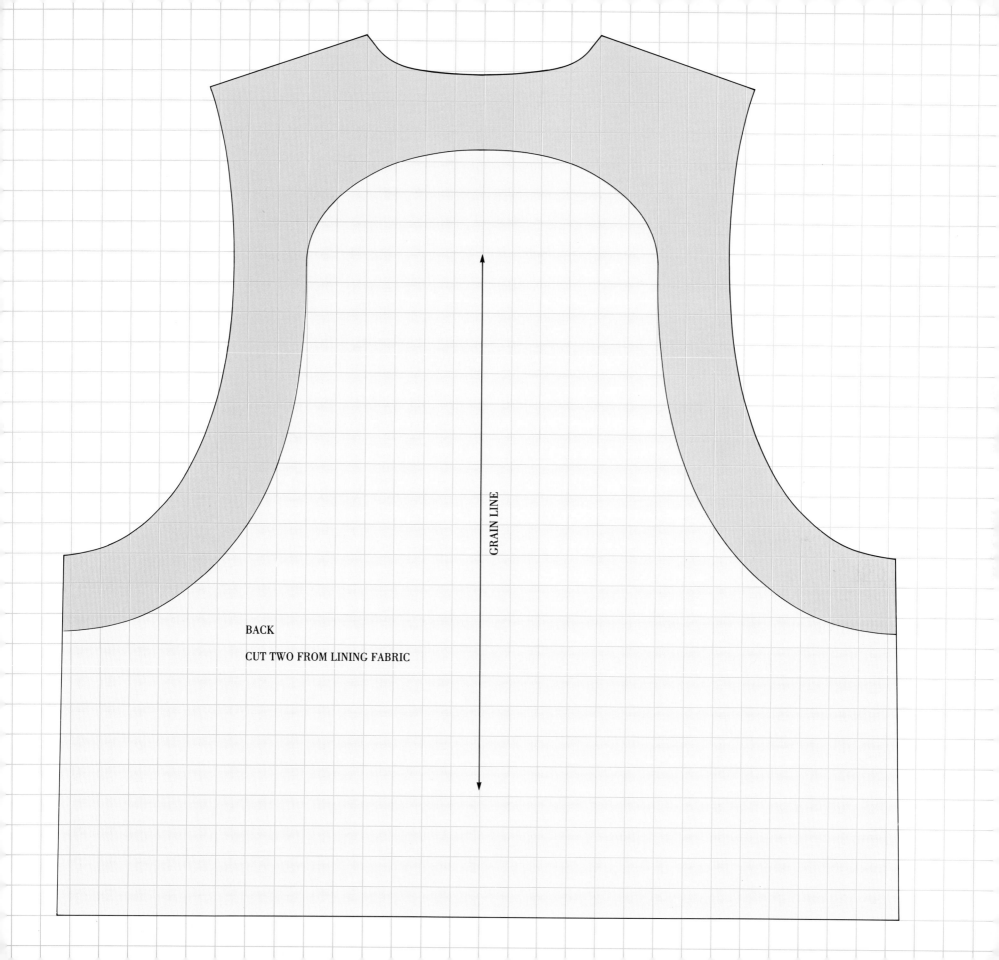

GRAIN LINE

BACK

CUT TWO FROM LINING FABRIC

SHIRT
Pages 78-79

LEFT SLEEVE

Centre — — — — — — — — — — — — — — *Centre*

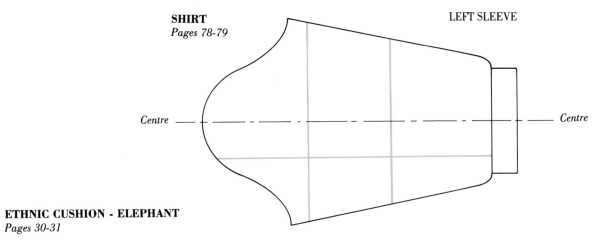

ETHNIC CUSHION - ELEPHANT
Pages 30-31

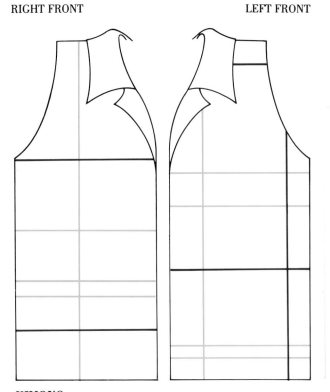

KIMONO
Pages 80-81

ENLARGE ON A PHOTOCOPIER BY 200%

Centre

BACK

TABLECLOTH
Pages 44-45

B C A

B

C

A

5 cm (2 in)

10.5 cm (4 in)

15 cm (6 in)

15 cm (6 in)

10.5 cm (4 in)

5 cm (2 in)

9.5 cm (3¾ in)

6.5 cm (2½ in)

4 cm (1½ in)

9.5 cm (3¾ in)

6.5 cm (2½ in)

4 cm (1½ in)

ETHNIC CUSHION - ZEBRA
Pages 30-31

Centre

RIGHT SLEEVE

Centre

ENLARGE ON A PHOTOCOPIER BY 200%

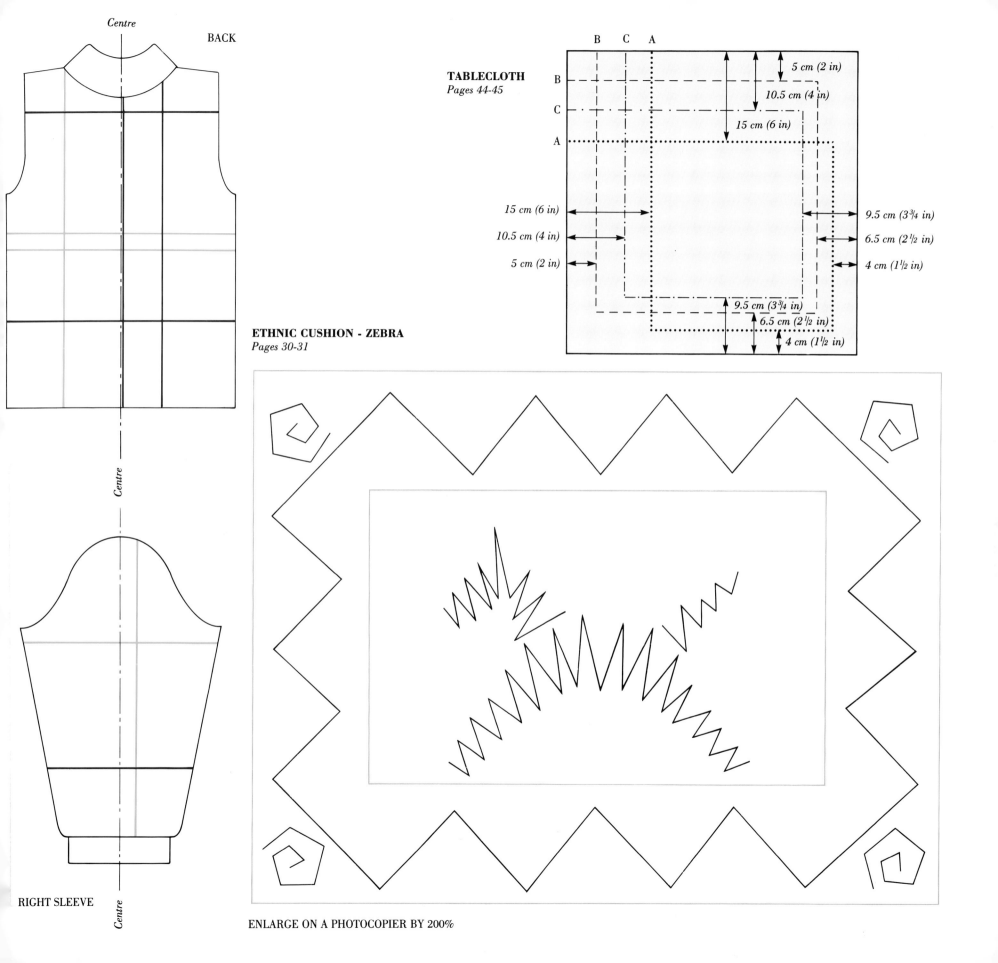

TARTAN THROW
Pages 26-27

■	*75 mm (3 in) wide tartan polyester 3.5 m (4 yd)*
■	*38 mm (1½ in) wide tartan polyester 4.5 m (5 yd)*
■	*50 mm (2 in) wide rust velvet 1.5 m (1¾ yd)*
■	*50 mm (2 in) wide green velvet 2.5 m (2¾ yd)*
■	*20 mm (¾ in) wide rust velvet 3.5 (4 yd)*
■	*20 mm (¾ in) wide green velvet 2 m (2¼ yd)*

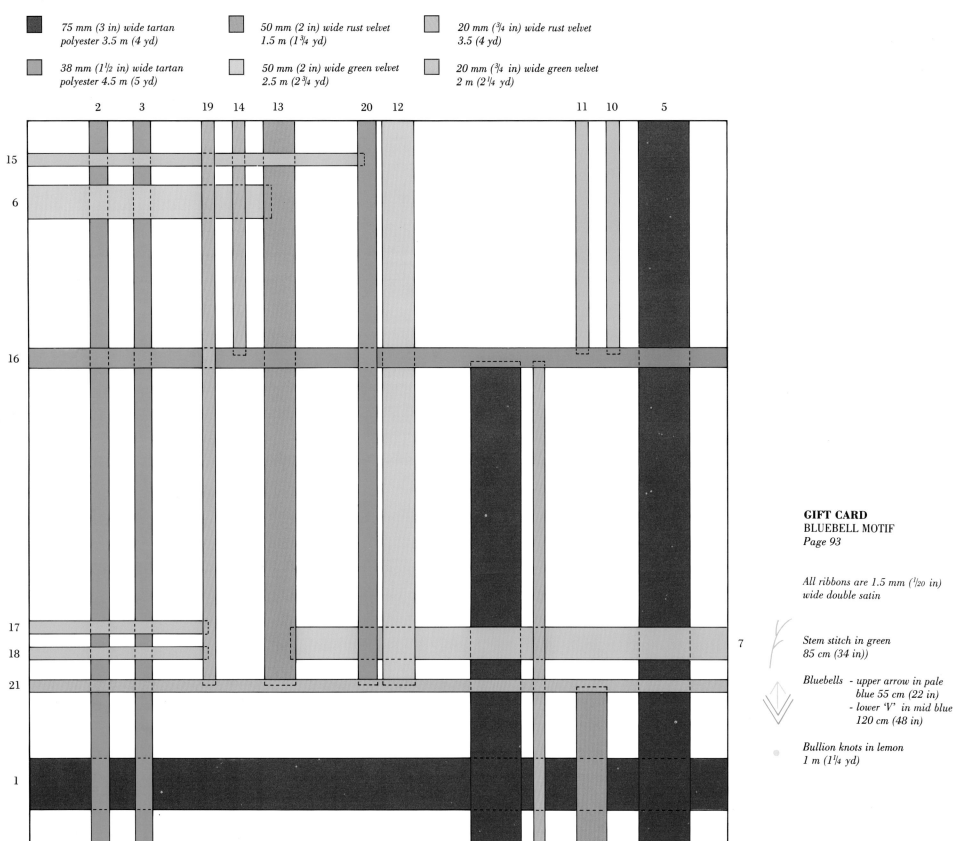

GIFT CARD
BLUEBELL MOTIF
Page 93

All ribbons are 1.5 mm (¹/20 in) wide double satin

Stem stitch in green 85 cm (34 in))

Bluebells - upper arrow in pale blue 55 cm (22 in)
*   - lower 'V' in mid blue 120 cm (48 in)*

Bullion knots in lemon 1 m (1¼ yd)

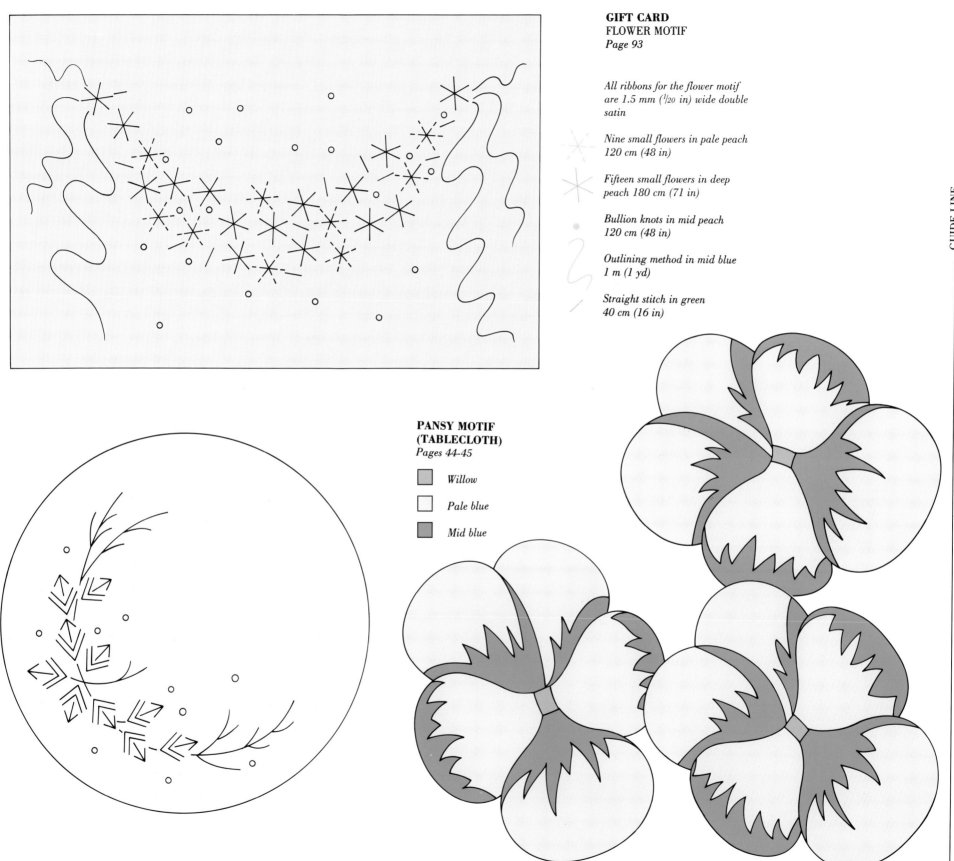

GIFT CARD
FLOWER MOTIF
Page 93

*All ribbons for the flower motif
are 1.5 mm (¹/₂₀ in) wide double
satin*

*Nine small flowers in pale peach
120 cm (48 in)*

*Fifteen small flowers in deep
peach 180 cm (71 in)*

*Bullion knots in mid peach
120 cm (48 in)*

*Outlining method in mid blue
1 m (1 yd)*

*Straight stitch in green
40 cm (16 in)*

**PANSY MOTIF
(TABLECLOTH)**
Pages 44-45

Willow

Pale blue

Mid blue

ENLARGE CHARTS A, B AND C ON A PHOTCOPIER BY 200%. CHART D IS GIVEN AS ACTUAL SIZE.

*All ribbons for the bedspread are
1.5 mm (¹/20 in) wide double satin*

CHART D

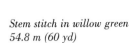

*Stem stitch in willow green
54.8 m (60 yd)*

*Large flowers - petals in wine
68.4 m (75 yd)
- knots in rose
39.4 m (44 yd)*

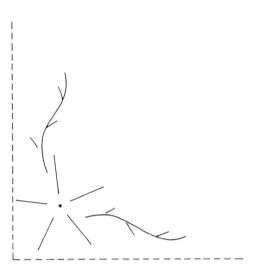

*Rosebuds   - upper arrow in
wine (see above)
- lower 'V' in rose
(see above)*

*Small flowers in dusky pink
20 m (22 yd)*

CHART A

CHART C

CHART B